Routledge Revivals

The Economic Problems of Europe

First Published in 1928 *The Economic Problems of Europe* presents a comprehensive overview of the economic and political transformation of Europe since the First World War. European and world problems often tend to be looked upon from the political, diplomatic, naval, or military aspect. Morgan Philips Price attempted to add the economic background and to show the connection between the political rearrangements since the First World War and the material needs of society, markets of the industrialist, the wages of the workman, and the loans of the bankers. He argued that with the growing internationalization of the world economy, the old map of the world is obsolete and the new one, if it is based on frontiers of finance and industry, will be something very different. This book is an essential read for scholars and researchers of economic history, war history, political economy, British economic history, and European history.

The Economic Problems of Europe
Pre-War and After

M. Philips Price

Routledge
Taylor & Francis Group

First published in 1928
by George Allen & Unwin Ltd

This edition first published in 2021 by Routledge
2 Park Square, Milton Park, Abingdon, Oxon, OX14 4RN
and by Routledge
605 Third Avenue, New York, NY 10017

Routledge is an imprint of the Taylor & Francis Group, an informa business

© M. Philips Price 1928

Publisher's Note
The publisher has gone to great lengths to ensure the quality of this reprint but points
out that some imperfections in the original copies may be apparent.

Disclaimer
The publisher has made every effort to trace copyright holders and welcomes
correspondence from those they have been unable to contact.

A Library of Congress record exists under LCCN: 29001839

ISBN: 978-1-032-15174-8(hbk)
ISBN: 978-1-003-24285-7(ebk)
ISBN: 978-1-032-15175-5(pbk)

Book DOI 10.4324/9781003242857

THE ECONOMIC
PROBLEMS OF EUROPE
PRE-WAR AND AFTER

By

M. PHILIPS PRICE

FOREWORD BY
THE RIGHT HON. SIDNEY WEBB, M.P.

LONDON
GEORGE ALLEN & UNWIN LTD
MUSEUM STREET

First published in 1928

Printed in Great Britain by
Unwin Brothers, Ltd., Woking

AUTHOR'S PREFACE

IN the following pages I have attempted to supply a gap in current literature. European and world problems tend to be looked upon from the political, diplomatic, naval, or military aspect. I have attempted to add the economic background and to show the connection between the political rearrangements since the war and the material needs of society, the markets of the industrialist, the wages of the workman, and the loans of the bankers. While collecting material for this book, I have been impressed by the increasing internationalization of world economy. The old map of the world is obsolete; the new one, if it is based on frontiers of finance and industry, will be something very different. In the light of this, how out of date do the speeches of European politicians of the old school seem to-day! Yet Europe is politically Balkanized, and the hunt for gold to found national currencies presents barriers to the new economic order, while the problem of armaments looms forbiddingly ahead. It is a race between the new in-rushing forces and the recuperative powers of the old.

I formed the conception of this book when preparing lectures for the National Labour Colleges, in 1925 and 1926, on the economic aspects of the Versailles Treaty and on the Dawes Plan. I soon saw, however, that I must extend the field of inquiry to include colonial problems and to the repercussions of America's financial policy abroad. Chapters VIII, IX, and X are amplified and extended from these lectures. I found also that no understanding of post-war European economy was possible without a review of its pre-war economy. I therefore devoted Chapters I to VIII to this subject, based on what has been published in the past and now largely out of print, together with other material collected by myself during my residence abroad. In this connection I have found useful material in the British Museum and in the Prussian State Library in Berlin. The last three chapters have been based on a careful perusal of contemporary publications in this and in continental countries, including Soviet Russia.

M. PHILIPS PRICE.

TAYNTON, GLOUCESTER;
February 2, 1928.

FOREWORD

THIS is a suggestive book, original in conception and novel in outlook, in which a series of problems of vital importance to Western Civilization are examined from an unfamiliar angle. As such, it deserves the unprejudiced consideration of economic and political students in Great Britain and the United States, and of statesmen everywhere. The almost unique experience of the author, during the past fifteen years, of the momentous changes still proceeding in the industrial and political organization of Central and Eastern Europe, lead him to inferences of importance as to some effects of the new "Industrial Revolution" which is taking place throughout the civilized world.

We stand to-day perplexed at the manifold problems which the Great War has revealed to the economist and the politician, apart from those which it has directly caused. Even to comprehend the nature of these problems demands an effort. We seem to be living in the midst of a rapidly developing transformation of industrial, financial, and social relations more far-reaching in its effects than the Industrial Revolution of the eighteenth century. A century ago the canal and the turnpike road, the steam-engine and the railway locomotive, the steamship and the cotton-gin, making available an enormous supply of a new raw material, changed, between 1750 and 1850, the whole face of Britain. This time the revolution is international and

world-wide. Who can measure the combined effects
on social life and economic organization, during the
years in which we are living, of such subversive transformations as are indicated by the novel applications
to industry of electricity and chemistry; the internal-
combustion engine; the spreading use of various
kinds of oil; the fixation of nitrogen from the atmosphere; the utilization of new plants, minerals and
alloys; the substitution of silk made out of woodpulp
for both cotton and wool; the increase in the magnitude
of factories, of ships and of business enterprises, and
of the general scale of production and of distributing
agencies; the new capital required in order to bring
up to date our iron and steel works, our engineering
factories, our railways, and other industries which
novel processes have left behind in the competitive
market; the internationalization, not only of finance,
but also of the direction of capital investments; the
almost miraculous revolutions in communication and
conveyance represented by the aeroplane, by broad-
casting, and by wireless telegraphy; and the vastly
heightened sensitiveness of the whole world caused by
the virtual simultaneity of news, opinions, and im-
pressions among the entire population? The social
historian of a hundred years hence will be better able
to gauge this twentieth-century Industrial Revolution
than those whose lives are buffeted by it. Unfortunately,
the present generation cannot wait for this future
historian. For my own part, I frankly avow that the
new complications baffle me. I doubt whether the
international problems now being raised are capable of

solution by the apparatus and methods of the nine-teenth-century economists. We need, if not more brains, at least a much more comprehensive detailed description of the facts than has hitherto been available. If Humanity is to control and direct the forces that it has unwittingly called into activity, it will require, not only more theory but also, and primarily, much more knowledge as to what is actually happening.

It is for this reason, and not because I pretend to have fathomed the world's problem in European reorganization, that I bespeak consideration for the attempt that Mr. Philips Price has made to expound and explain what seems to him to be happening in the economic and political transformations that are proceeding whilst the politicians are talking.

SIDNEY WEBB.

PASSFIELD CORNER,
LIPHOOK, HANTS,
May 1928.

CONTENTS

THE ECONOMIC PROBLEMS OF EUROPE

PRE-WAR AND AFTER

CHAPTER I

PAST CRISES IN ENGLISH INDUSTRIAL HISTORY

IF anyone living to-day were to have a glimpse of Imperial Rome during the last stages of her decline, I doubt if he would gather the impression that the world was undergoing a great change. He would probably see the common folk living their private lives, enjoying their pleasures, enduring their troubles, without forethought of anything important happening to the basis of the society in which they lived. Historians have hitherto been apt to lay stress on the dramatic events, which every now and then may have fixed the attention of contemporary public opinion, and not enough on the long periods of workaday life which the average citizen of ancient society must have been leading. No doubt the absence of newspapers and the imperfect means of communication contributed towards our difficulty in getting any clear idea of the social life of past times. Still, one cannot help feeling that it is more important to know, for instance, about the state of British agriculture in the time of King Alfred than it is to know about the story of his burnt cakes. But the rise or fall of social systems in the past has been spread out over decades, and often centuries, and, though punctuated by catastrophic episodes, the slowness of the process has prevented the contemporary citizen from perceiving the general trend of events. Hence records of the most interesting part of history are scarce.

Coming to later times, it is, for example, very difficult to say in our history when the feudal system ended and the basis of modern forms of production and exchange came into being. The centuries are punctuated with certain convulsive episodes, like the seizure of the monastic lands by Henry VIII, the enclosures of the commons in Elizabeth's time, the Civil War and the Commonwealth, the struggle with the Pretenders, the French wars, the repressions of Pitt, and the Luddite and Chartist movements. But in between the manifestations of violent coercion are long periods of apparently quiet growth of society, indicated, for example, by the Elizabethan Poor Law, the various gradual methods by which Parliament got control over the nation's finances, the growth of popular representation and the coming of trade unionism. A person living through these times would not suppose that any very fundamental economic change was taking place. But, looking back on these centuries, we can see that one society was being replaced by another. Thus at the beginning of the period when feudalism was in the decline people were classified socially according to birth and to the amount of land and serfs they possessed. At the end of it they were divided according to the amount of marketable goods, or machines for producing them, which they possessed. The revolution had been accomplished. There had been forceful episodes in its progress. But man's ways are like Nature's ways; a river flowing from the mountains to the sea has rapids, and sometimes cascades interspersed with limpid pools and quiet reaches.

It is possible to fix on certain dates and mark them as historical signposts, indicating the point of time at which the pace of evolution slackened or accelerated. They are generally events of a revolutionary or counter-revolutionary nature. Such dates of accelerated speed were the years 1789–1792 in France, the Civil War (1642–1649), the landing of William of Orange (1688), the Reform Bill (1832) in England, in Russia (1917–1918). For slackened speed the Restoration of the Stuarts, the Congress of Vienna, the accession of Alexander III in Russia are prominent examples. But the accession of Charles II did not prevent the seeds being sown which led to the Revolution of 1688. It represented the last attempt of a Scottish dynasty steeped in the feudalism of the Middle Ages to prevent the growth of the influence of Dutch mercantilism and finance over England. The Russian Communist Revolution of 1917 did not prevent the seeds being sown which made possible the compromise of 1921, the New Economic Policy and Lenin's alliance between workman and peasant. These revolutionary and counter-revolutionary episodes became merely the points at which the evolutionary currents either flowed faster or became more sluggish.

Our survey in the following pages will concern mainly Europe in general and England in particular. But for this purpose we must consider the relations of Europe with America and with the colonial areas of Asia and Africa. Moreover, if we are to analyse effectively the state of Europe to-day, we must go down to the roots from which contemporary society has grown. We must realize first that all the great events of the past and of our time have taken place within the framework of, and have in part been conditioned by, the material surroundings under which man has had to win his livelihood from Nature. If, therefore, we are passing through a period of social and political crisis, there must be some economic adjustments going on beneath the surface. We all agree that society in Europe has been passing through a state of crisis since the end of the Great War. But crises of one sort or another have always been a feature of past history. They have been going on ever since the economic system based on private capital emerged from a system based on feudal tenure of land. The best way to test the pulse of the system that arose out of feudal society and is best known as capitalistic society is by foreign trade returns. This at least is true of the early stages of that society. Let us take England as our example. Here, in the course of time, an industrial system has come into being, which exists by producing more of certain lines of goods than can be consumed at home and by exchanging them for what it cannot produce. This foreign trade is a distinctive feature of the system of private capital which followed the feudal system. It has enabled a small agricultural and sheep-raising country, as England once was, to become a great industrial country, buying three-quarters of its food abroad and paying for it by the export of technical services, manufactured goods and banking credits. The surplus commodities available for export and the resultant foreign trade, therefore, were in the early stages of capitalistic society good indications of the prosperity of the country.

Now if one takes the foreign trade returns of Britain and examines them as far back as we can go till 1783—that is, for 144 years—we can plot a curve which begins in 1785 at £2 per head of population and reaches £30 per head in 1913 in a steadily rising incline. But if the curve is examined more carefully it will be observed that it is not even. There are sharp fluctuations which indicate minor booms and depressions, and which vary from four to twelve years in duration and average out at somewhere about eight years. In addition to this, one can observe that there are greater undulations spreading over periods of, roughly, twenty to twenty-five years, of which the smaller undulations are like ripples on an Atlantic swell. Thus from 1800 to 1820 the curve was, apart from the smaller undulations, falling slightly. From 1820 to 1848 the gradual recovery of the English economic system from the Napoleonic wars was indicated in a very gradual rise of the curve, which reached in 1848 £10 per head of population. England was beginning to reap the benefits of the political upheavals of former generations. If the eighteenth century had been a period of apparent stagnation, it was also a period of quiet consolidation. The political gains of the Civil War period, 1642–1649, and of the Revolution of 1688, were taking material shape in the founding of new industries, the early textile trades, hand-weaving and small machine crafts, while the energy of Coke of Norfolk and others brought improved machinery and methods of breeding and cultivation to British agriculture. The introduction of the use of steam at the end of the eighteenth century was followed by the discovery of new methods of smelting iron, and enterprising citizens were developing mines and establishing the factory system in which wage-earners worked for a miserable pittance. And so the vested interests in the new factory industries of the late Georgian and early Victorian times came into conflict with a political system which still gave large privileges to agrarian landlords.

But the floodgates which squirearchy had set up to stem the flood of progress burst, first in the Reform

Bill of 1832 and then, fifteen years later, when the Corn Laws were repealed. The full stream of private capital accumulations from industrial processes was let loose. The foreign trade returns rose from £12 per head of population in 1852 to £21 per head in 1873, with, as mentioned above, smaller cycles of roughly eight years. Then set in a period of depression in the eighties, when the foreign trade returns fell to £17 in 1888. Foreign competition in the textile trades began to be felt after the Franco-Prussian War. Britain had been the exporter of cotton goods all over the world. Such had been the wealth and influence of Lancashire's staple industry that Manchester had given the tone to English politics since the days when, in 1847, the Whig manufacturers had short-circuited the Chartist revolutionary current by repealing the Corn Laws. Now not only were there other textile competitors in France and Germany, but the discovery of the methods of smelting new alloys of iron and of manufacturing steel in various forms had opened out great possibilities of expanding engineering trades. Birmingham became the pacemaker of British politics from the eighties onwards. The export of engineering goods, indeed, had become a necessity for England to enable her to balance her large import bill. But engineering goods required concessions abroad to construct railways, harbours, and factories, and involved relations with foreign Governments and peoples. The policy of *laissez-faire* in foreign affairs gave way to a policy of direct interference in the affairs of other countries. Splendid isolation was now economically out of date and modern Imperialism started on its course. The capital engaged in making goods which were speedily consumed, like textiles, and which needed only open markets and freedom of trade, was being replaced in the political councils of the nations, and particularly of England, by capital engaged in the manufacture of goods that produced other goods and which only depreciated slowly. "Constructional" capital was replacing "consumption" capital. It is no accident, therefore, that at this period of English history the Liberal Party split into two contending factions, and that the Manchester Free Trade policy, hitherto unchallenged, was met by the policy of Birmingham—Protection and Colonial Expansion.

Thus, early in the nineties, and thanks very largely to "Birminghamism," the indicators of foreign trade showed a rise again, and it rose from £18 per head of population in 1894 to £30 per head in 1913, not counting the average eight years' fluctuation in between. British constructional capital was pushing and developing its spheres of influence all over the world, and large accumulations were being made in the home country from investments in Indian railways, South American harbours, West African palm-oil forests, Malayan rubber, and Canadian ranches. The development of South African mines increased the gold supply of the world and caused a rise in world prices, and hence improving trade. The son of a humble Scotchman had traversed Africa from sea to sea, had pierced the jungle and, with religion as his aid, had begun to break down human slavery and open the way to the partition of Africa by the Great Powers. Livingstone, although he did not know it, was the instrument of a new social order, breaking down the ancient society of the Dark Continent. Soon the thunder of the guns at Majuba Hill told that the new form of capital did not operate in the undeveloped parts of the earth without the shedding of human blood. The gold and diamond interests were concerned with the removal of the rights of older settlers in the exploitation of these treasures. "Manchesterism" had fought a war with China to make her people *consume* opium. "Birminghamism" fought a war with the Boers to make them *construct* railways, made from the metals of the English Black Country, to serve the mines. And so the export of engineering construction goods went on apace to develop the produce and minerals of Asia, Africa, and South America.

In the old days of mercantile buccaneering, trade followed the flag. But in the Manchester period of textile supremacy and in the Birmingham period of metal-ware supremacy foreign trade did not necessarily need the flag at all. It did not require the Union Jack to fly in China in order to sell cotton goods there. Guns at Hongkong and a blockade of the Yang-tse were enough to secure what was needed, and the Dragon flag could fly on the Imperial Palaces at Peking without disturbing the flow of British goods to the Far East. British railways could also be constructed in the Argentine, which was not a part of the British Empire. But the export of constructional goods, though not bound to the flag, relied increasingly on the banker to give the artificial buying power to the natives of the colonial lands to enable them to use the railways, harbours, and public works which Birmingham had constructed for them. The flag was no longer the pioneer, as it was in the days of Drake and the Spanish Main. The flag followed up the blazed trail as part of the baggage train. The pioneer was cash and banking credit. In other words, trade now followed the cash.

And so it comes about that the capital investments abroad of the older countries are the decisive factor in the growth of international trade. We noted above the periods of prosperity and crisis in the rising fortunes of England's industries in the nineteenth century. And we chose as our indicator, to measure the pulse of industry and commerce, the foreign trade returns; that is, the quantity and value of the goods entering and leaving the shores of this country. But with the coming of "construction" capital these figures become increasingly less reliable as an indicator of crisis and prosperity. The building of networks of railways in a colony may cause a large export of machinery on credit from an old industrial country, bringing, perhaps for some years, no corresponding import of goods back from the colony. There will, then, be an export surplus for the old country and an import surplus for the colony. But after a time, when the new railways have begun to have their effect on the native economy, the colony may become a large grain or raw material exporting area, and the banks who have financed the railways will have control over the credit which finances the import into the old country of the food and raw material from the colony. They will sell this produce, and the cash received will become, from the standpoint of national economy, interest on the capital invested in the railways—a kind of tribute levied or reparation paid, upon which there is no return payment by the old country. Consequently the trade returns of the old country tend to become passive, import exceeding export, while those of the colony tend to become active, export exceeding import. Examples of this could have been found in the early development of the African Crown Colonies, which had originally passive trade balances and now have in some cases active ones. Britain herself naturally has a large passive trade balance, which is caused by the "invisible" exports in the form of capital for which interest is paid in food and raw material by agrarian and tropical countries. It follows from all this that trade returns to-day by themselves will not tell us much about the state of trade and industry in a country or about the health or otherwise of the social system based on the accumulation of fortunes in the hands of private individuals. The important factor which has to be known to-day in evaluating the prosperity or otherwise of the economic system of a country is the "invisible" export of capital invested outside a country, causing an apparent inequality in the imports and exports. For that reason, if we want to see how the national economy of Great Britain is faring under our present social system and distribution of wealth, we must study, not the trade returns only, but also the investment of capital outside the country, its rate of increase and its geographical direction.

The problem has been stated in concise language by Sir Josiah Stamp in a lecture delivered in 1926 to the Huddersfield Chamber of Commerce. Referring to the nature of the exports of a given country, he said that "they could be divided into two sections, the first and larger part linked up automatically and arithmetically with the volume of imports which together he called national barter ; and the second and smaller part quite independent of the total volume of this interchange trade." In the case of the first type of export "there was complete equivalence between the imports and exports. . . . Every purchase of an import brought about a sale of an export, or conversely." Sir Josiah was here clearly thinking of the type of trade which developed before the war and is to some extent now again between Britain and Germany. Neither is an undeveloped colonial country. Both are highly industrialized and depend for an economic balance and for food and raw material on the sale of manufactured goods and investment of capital abroad. The large Anglo-German trade was a direct exchange of similar types of articles. German engineering industries specialized in some technical processes more than in others, and the same thing applied to British industries. The interchange of these articles was of mutual advantage and did not represent a change in the economy of either country such as results when machinery is sent to a colony to develop railways.

Sir Josiah then went on: "The second or smaller part of the volume of foreign trade was quite independent of the interchange section and had its own limits. He called it the investment volume, and it represented the export or import surplus, according to whether the interest on capital invested abroad was more or less than the new capital movements. It did not necessarily fluctuate with the total trade, and might be constant whether the interchange trade was represented by A plus B or 3A plus 3B. But whatever it was, its limit was the limit of real savings after deducting home investment. . . . Except in the case of reparation or interest payments secured out of taxation, it was impossible to get an export surplus by mere activity of export industries *unbacked by capital accumulation by the nation as a whole.*" (My italics.)

This confirms the argument advanced above that capital invested in industry in the older countries to-day produces goods a portion of which are exported to undeveloped countries and are not paid for at once, but the interest on them accumulates and returns in goods, generally food and raw material, later. Sometimes it even takes the form of the older country granting purchasing power to the colonial country; in other words, exporting banking capital or credit to it and permitting it to use that credit to purchase goods, not from the country that granted the credit, but from a third one. Generally, however, the financial houses exporting such credit are interested, directly or indirectly, in industrial processes in the old country and make it a condition of the transaction that the goods be bought at the source of origin of the credit.

Sir Josiah regards the goods and credit thus exported as the smaller part of the total trade. He says: "Before the war our investments abroad roughly cancelled our interest due from abroad. Our imports and exports of goods and services virtually balanced, and it was quite possible that our total foreign trade was no different in volume from what it would have been if we had never made any foreign investments at all. The export surplus of 1925 was put as low as £28 millions, but although this might mean less prosperity for export trades, it was not necessarily a national calamity if home investment was considerable." It thus appears that before the war Britain's "interchange" trade balanced in export and import, and that the passive trade balance of those years was not due to an unfavourable balance of the former, but due to the lending abroad of surplus profits saved from the "interchange" trade. These savings lent abroad were the real invisible exports which raised the visible imports above the visible exports. Sir Josiah seems to regard some of this "investment" trade as superfluous, at least before the war, for Britain. I return to this question in a later chapter. Suffice it to say here that it was just that section of society, interested in this investment trade, that used the largest influence and brought the biggest pressure to bear on the foreign policy of the country. This investment capital may have been a relatively small stone in the pre-war economy of the Old World, but it held up the arch on which was based the foreign policy, diplomatic activity, military and naval strategy of the Powers of Europe. In order, therefore, to study the nature of the contemporary crisis in European economy it is worth examining the form and direction of the capital investments of the principal European countries from early times, beginning with Great Britain.

CHAPTER II

EARLY PHASE OF BRITISH CAPITAL INVEST-MENTS; ENGLAND A DEBTOR STATE

THE distinctive feature of the British Empire is the diversity of its forms of society and of the economic structure of its loosely knit component parts. Being a maritime empire, its founders were explorers who traversed the seas and planted settlements in every kind of climate and amidst every kind of human society. The result was the evolution of such countries as Canada on the one hand and Nigeria on the other. The Empire was not pieced together systematically like the old Russian Empire. It just "happened." But in spite of its anarchical beginnings the law of evolution of human society and the ever-growing complexity of human economy can be traced in its structure throughout the decades of its history.

We may as well set aside at once all sentimental talk about high ideals and desire to improve the condition of the natives in heathen lands as the incentive to colonization of the British Empire. The simple facts are that the British Empire, like every other organization for the amassing of material wealth, was particularly successful because it was the first in the field, and because the centre from which the organization radiated was geographically very well situated at the junction of many sea routes. The feudal system was steadily decaying from the fifteenth century onwards. Into the cause of its decay we need not enter here, but we will just note that its distinctive feature was the existence of self-sufficient agrarian communities, cultivating land on the three-field system with extensive common lands and paying tribute to military overlords who defended them from nomadic incursions from Asia and Scandinavia. Trade was confined largely to luxuries of the overlords.

The early forms of capital accumulation coincided with the beginnings of trade in articles of more general consumption than those which had been the case hitherto. There is little doubt that improvement in the methods of preparing wool for human clothing was largely responsible for the growth of a trade between the West of Europe and the East which arose about the sixteenth century and resulted in the exchange of textile and woollen goods for silks, spices, and precious wares. The growth of this exchange gradually gave increased economic influence to those members of the community who handled these goods, and with this came an increase of political power. It is no accident that the new type of merchant capitalists began to appear and to gain increasing hold over the Governments of the States of Europe on its Western seaboard —namely, Holland, Britain, Spain, and Portugal. The power of mercantile capital had been in existence for years before the sixteenth century. The merchants in the trading republics of Northern Italy had been lending money to feudal princes to enable them to carry on wars, and to speculate with the agrarian produce of their subjects, as far back as the fourteenth century. The Florentine merchants in particular had lent considerable sums of money to Henry V of England on the security of the English customs. But with the discovery of the compass and the improvement in the arts of navigation of the high seas the economic, and with it the political, power in Europe shifted from the inland Mediterranean coasts to the Atlantic seaboard.

We thus see in the countries along this seaboard

the rise of merchant princes, laying the foundations of empires of later days. Mercantile Imperialism of these times took two forms. It took the form of sending out goods in ships to some foreign potentate and advancing them to him on credit. This kind of trade proved lucrative in the East, where in exchange for goods on credit the merchants were able to get a monopoly of the import of colonial produce to the home land. In this way the British and Dutch Empires were built up in Asia. As far back as the sixteenth century Queen Elizabeth granted the first Charter to the Levant Company in London for trade with Turkey, and to the East India Company for trade with India. Subsequently the East India Company, through the economic power of loans and military force, to act as guarantees for the monopolies arising from these loans, acquired political power and replaced the native rulers in fact if not in name. The other form of Mercantile Imperialism was more prevalent on the American continent. British and Spanish merchant buccaneers set out across the Atlantic, and on arrival in the new lands settled there and made plantations of cotton, sugar, and tobacco, which they then imported to the home country. This was a case of direct settlement of Europeans in the colony, and, finding no ancient civilization with native potentates in control, they set to work to directly subjugate the natives and to harness their labour to the plantations which they had made. Here was not a case of bribery or cajolery, followed by diplomatic action and force, but simply of force from the beginning. In Asia it was a case of mercantile capital harnessing an ancient feudal hierarchy with its serfs and independent cultivators to its system of foreign exchange. In America it was a case of mercantile capital harnessing an even older form of society—a primitive tribal and hunting society—to its economic system. It is not difficult to see that in the latter case it was very easy for a system of direct chattel slavery to develop, of the same kind as existed centuries before in the Roman Empire and over which the system of serfdom in the feudal system of the Middle Ages was a considerable advance, when judged from the human and moral standpoint. Mercantile Imperialism on the American continent has a black chapter to its record, for the plantations across the Atlantic became soon manned by African negroes bought and sold like cattle and transplanted from their native homes. Coloured labourers became once more domestic livestock, like cattle and horses.

Arising out of this difference between the type of early colonial Imperialism in Asia on the one hand and in America on the other, there developed a difference in the type of capital investment of the Mother Country in these areas. We set out in this chapter to study the growth of British capital export in undeveloped lands, and we find that in Asia the capital invested abroad in the early days of mercantile capital was almost entirely in the transport trade in goods. The London and Amsterdam merchants did not at first seize lands in Asia, acquire native slaves, and proceed to make plantations. Production in tropical lands was carried out partly by native rulers with serfs and partly by independent cultivators. The European merchants of the East India Company only invested their money in ships and in the goods which they sent out there in exchange for the tropical produce. In the Americas, on the other hand, the system of direct investment of capital from the Mother Country in the plantations of these colonies went on from the first. Large quantities of capital went from Europe to develop these plantations all through the seventeenth century. The London Company was particularly active in Virginia during this time, and raised loans for their plantation enterprises. These took the form of sending out equipment for cultivating land, building houses, stores, barns. In other words, while the East India Company was exporting and importing only consumable goods and providing the shipping accommodation, the New England planter was already importing into the colony constructional goods which only after a few years would yield produce to be imported to the Mother Country. This was a more advanced state of capitalistic Imperialism. Countries with a high form of production generally begin their relations with countries of backward economy by forcing the latter to increase their production by adopting new and more efficient methods. This stage then carries with it the necessity of exporting constructional goods to the colony, and it was reached a century or more earlier in the American than in the Asiatic colonies. The ancient civilization of the East set a brake on the transformation of mercantile capitalism into the early forms of constructional capitalism.

As a matter of fact, England at this time was not in the main a capital-exporting but rather a capital-importing land. Dutch capital was invested in England to a large extent all through the seventeenth century. It largely rebuilt London after the Fire; it largely drained the Fens. The development of English towns and small industries, the improving and enclosing of land, went on all through the seventeenth century and at a slower rate in the eighteenth century. In 1774, nevertheless, England was paying to Holland £1 million a year interest on capital borrowed, and the total debt to Holland at this time amounted to about £25 millions. But by the beginning of the eighteenth century England was ceasing to be an undeveloped back-garden of Europe. It was advancing along the road of progress, albeit by a painful process, as witness the gangs of ragged unemployed on the roads, dispossessed of their native land by enclosing landlords. The bleating of sheep in the great ranches was heard where once the woods resounded to the sturdy stroke of British sons of the soil. The Elizabethan Poor Law was now the custodian of their fortunes. And so England, having been "developed" by the Dutch bankers and financiers, started on the road of "developing" other countries. The era of Dutch financiers was passing. A German king sat on the English throne in place of a Dutch one. The rising merchant class of London preferred a petty reactionary, feudal German prince to a nominee of the Amsterdam bankers, although they found that they got more than they bargained for when George III tried to revive the tradition of the "divine right of kings."

The eighteenth century was marked by a flow of British capital investments to the colonies. The rate of investment to the Americas which had been going on in the seventeenth was continued at a greater rate in the eighteenth. But now it began to go to the Asiatic colonies as well, and the East India Company began to borrow in London to develop mines and estates in India and the East. London became a centre for foreign investment. At first, it is true, it was not very successful. Bubble companies, the most famous of which was that of the South Sea, were launched, inflated, and burst. The theory was being actively propagated, in Paris as well as in London, that national debts could be liquidated by farming out colonial monopolies to private companies of merchants in payment of part of the profits to the State. John

Law preached this idea at the Court of Louis XIV. The hunt for colonial possessions was redoubled, resulting in a whole series of wars. The War of Spanish Succession and the Seven Years' War was not entirely due to the quarrels of Royalties over mistresses. As a result of the former war England gained Gibraltar, the key to India, and as a result of the second Prussia was used by England to weaken Austria and to prevent her from launching out on a colonial policy from her point of vantage in the Netherlands.

The new colonies which England acquired in the eighteenth century gave a great impetus to scientific invention and paved the way for the industrial revolution. The markets for increased production were now there. Canada had been wrested from the French. The East India Company had most of the native rulers of India under its indirect, and some territories under its direct, control. The problem now was to raise production at home to supply these potential markets. It was this atmosphere that created the conditions favourable for scientific inventions. Steam power was to turn out by the thousands goods formerly turned out by hand by the hundred. In the second half of the eighteenth century a change in British trade took place indicating a change in the direction of capital investments. Up till then large British exports in wool and raw material had gone to Holland, largely to pay the £1 million debt to the Amsterdam banks. Now the tendencies for British exports was to the new colonies, and took the form more of manufactured and partly manufactured goods. The exports to Holland, meanwhile, became relatively less. This indicated that the debt of the colonies to London was rising and the debt of London to Amsterdam was relatively declining.

Towards the end of the eighteenth century a temporary, if serious, set-back was experienced by British mercantile and industrial capital. A movement for independence arose in the colonies and resulted ultimately in political separation. The whole basis of the operation of West European capital in America, Africa, and Asia had been one of monopoly. In Africa and Asia there was little or no resistance to this. India, as we have seen, could be harnessed to the system by a judicious mixture of corruption and force. But there arose there during the last half of the eighteenth century a class of Anglo-Indian administrators in the service of the East India Company. They were lent by the Home Government, which was concerned not only with trade monopoly but also with the interests of the natives. The new class of colonial administrators in Asia developed a more far-seeing policy of protection of native rights, in response to the influence of the Government at home, and was not inclined to provide soldiers, ships, and money without some sort of control over the operations of mercantile capital in these areas. This was apparently the historical significance of the Warren Hastings trial, and of the continuous conflict that went on till right into the nineteenth century between the East India Company and the Government in London. The somewhat more far-sighted policy of the Home Government, coupled with the absence of any independent white settlers in the East, prevented developments which might have led to a breakaway of the Asiatic part of the British Empire. But in the African and American colonies the position was different. Here the natives were, as we have seen above, living in primitive tribal conditions, and moreover the climate made it possible for parts at any rate of both continents to be inhabited by white settlers. Hence in Cape Colony

C

and the Transvaal, in Canada, New England, Virginia, the Carolinas and Brazil, white colonists of Western Europe, British, French, Spanish, and Portuguese, settled on estates in these areas and started cultivation of products for import to Europe. These white colonists began in the last half of the eighteenth century to chafe under the exorbitant monopolies of the vested interests in London, Paris, Madrid, and Lisbon. The latter wanted to force their wares on the colonists at their own prices. They wanted also to control the slave trade between Africa and America. Some wanted to keep all the profits on the slave trade in London. Others were raising voices for its abolition. All these factors combined to swell the stream which demanded freedom of trading restrictions and the end of interference in the domestic affairs of the colonies on the part of the Home Governments. The movement was not confined to the colonies under British control. The Spanish colonies in South America were also affected by the movement for independence. Spain had to abandon her restrictive trade monopolies and gradually permit freedom of trade between Europe and her South American colonies. Later they severed political connection as well. In Africa the Dutch colonists in the Cape Colony made the famous trek across the Orange River and founded the Transvaal Republics about this time, in response to the same desire to be freed of oppressive economic restriction of the Motherland. But the biggest convulsion of all came in the New England colonies from the desire of the American colonists to break through the monopolies imposed by the London merchants on all goods imported into Boston harbour. The incident with the Boston tea was the spark which helped to start the flame of civil war. The humiliation of England and the founding of the independent North

American Republic temporarily hit British mercantile capital. Not only did the export of goods to America decline, but British capital, which had begun to flow in a regular stream to develop the plantations of English settlers out there, ceased to flow. The development of the American estates was carried on then partly by the French and partly by the Dutch, but in the last decade of the eighteenth century the great social convulsion in France restricted all export of capital across the Atlantic from that quarter. Amsterdam remained, as it was all through this century, the financial centre of the world, but its exports of capital went principally to the East. With France now paralysed by the Revolution, the struggle for supremacy rested with London and Amsterdam.

BIBLIOGRAPHY

Cambridge Modern History.
Akkumulation des Kapitals, by Rosa Luxemburg. Leipzig, Frankes Verlag, 1921.
English Economic History, Selected Documents by Bland, Brown, and Tawney. Ball & Sons.
Industrial History of England, by Gibbins. Methuen & Co.

CHAPTER III

BRITISH CAPITAL EXPORTS IN THE NINETEENTH
CENTURY; ENGLAND A CREDITOR STATE

THE Napoleonic wars proved the undoing of Amsterdam as the monetary centre of the world. The military occupation of the Netherlands by the French armies and the declaration of the continental economic system, whereby England was blockaded, prevented financial intercourse of Amsterdam with the overseas colonies as long as England had command of the seas. So the export of capital from Holland dwindled during these years to nothing. England, however, was hit hardly less severely. All the available capital accumulations in the country were absorbed for the war with France, so that nothing was left to go abroad. London still held eighty million dollars of American loans, mostly contracted for the development of estates prior to the War of Independence.[1] These loans were still held in London during the Napoleonic wars. But in the main England was during these years more a capital-importing than a capital-exporting land. *Émigrés* and members of the old French aristocracy had in these troublous times transferred what wealth they could save from the holocaust in France to London. In 1810, £18 millions of the British National Debt were held by foreigners and, as such, were exempt from taxation.[2]

After the fall of Napoleon and the end of the war, the French *émigrés* gradually began to withdraw their balances from London, while accumulations of

[1] *Export of Capital*, by C. K. Hobson.
[2] *Wealth of Nations*, Adam Smith, vol. i. p. 93.

savings began to seek outlets in foreign investments once more. Then it was seen that London was quickly forging ahead of Amsterdam, whose bankers never really recovered the ground they lost from the Napoleonic wars. Now, indeed, there began a considerable amount of foreign borrowing in different parts of the world. Most of the Western European Governments were either in a bankrupt or in a semi-insolvent state. They came to London, where profits from pre-war colonial investments were beginning to accumulate again, and to provide a fund from which fresh investments could be made. Thus in 1817 and 1818 the London Stock Exchange provided £38 millions in loans to the Governments of vanquished France and victorious Prussia, Austria, and Russia. France, being the most needy, got the lion's share, viz. £27 millions at from 7½ per cent. to 9½ per cent. This was the "Dawes loan" of the early nineteenth century to stabilize the currency and restart on its legs again a defeated foe. For which piece of philanthropy a goodly interest was duly taken. Between 1818 and 1825 further loans to the tune of £31 millions were borrowed by European Governments in London. The other direction into which British capital investments were moving at this time was the United States. Between 1818 and 1825 £18 millions in loans went to the United States Government and municipalities from London and to private undertakings and estates. Public development schemes were now taking shape in America, and canals and harbours were being built, largely with British capital.[1] Soon after 1820 a movement of capital from England began to the South American countries which were winning their political independence. By 1825 £38 millions

[1] *Statistical Illustrations of the British Empire*, London Statistical Society, 1827, p. 112.

were raised in London for mining development in these countries. But speculation began to exceed reasonable bounds and mining companies' capital was soon watered. A crisis took place in that year, and much of this capital was lost.

After 1825 several continental countries began to set up their own industries. But in order to get started they came to London for money and to Birmingham and Manchester for equipment and machinery. France, Belgium, Austria, and the German States began setting up textile factories, mills, and metal shops of all kinds with the aid of British capital, British artisans and skilled engineers. The same thing went on in the United States, where British citizens and capital went out to develop industries. In the latter case the bulk of those who went out seldom returned to their native land, but remained and became United States citizens.

Thus in the thirties and forties of the nineteenth century there were two main directions of export of British capital—one towards the European continent and the other towards the United States. The object for which the foreign investments were made was (1) to stabilize the currency of Governments and restore financial solvency after the wars at the beginning of the century; (2) to develop transport and new industries in these countries, which industrially were several decades behind Britain. The first tended to create a bondholding class, holding fixed-interest bearing securities; the second a more speculative investor, earning high dividends from foreign industrial concessions. As far as we can see, the amounts invested by both types of capitalist in England were about the same. In 1840 the amount of United States public debt held by British citizens was £40 millions, and about an equal sum of public debts of the European continental countries was similarly held. Between 1833 and 1845 a little over £50 millions were subscribed by British investors for railway undertakings in Belgium, France, Germany, and the United States. A further sum, probably slightly less than £50 millions, went to these countries from England for general industrial purposes and for the development of estates. The largest amount was absorbed by the railway booms, which came in the United States and on the Continent about ten years later than in England. This was an age in which the inventions of Watt and Stephenson were being commercialized on a very large scale, and capital savings were rapidly flowing into undertakings which revolutionized transport, thanks to these scientific inventions. As soon as the home country had been covered by a network of railways, capital began to be exported to North America and the continent for the exploitation of the new inventions over there.

After the middle of the century a tendency began to develop in the colonial or capital-importing countries which had an important effect upon later developments. Both in the United States and in Canada a movement for the imposition of tariffs on imported manufactured goods arose. Hitherto Lancashire textile goods and Birmingham machinery had enjoyed a free market everywhere. But the growth of manufacturing industry in the new countries brought with it repercussions on the home or capital-exporting country. In 1859 Canada acquired the right, and exercised it, of imposing duties on foreign goods, including British. The United States had been doing so for some time, and after the Franco-Prussian War the new German Empire, which industrially was still a colonial and undeveloped area, established its Zollverein. This caused the theorists and economists of the Victorian Age to reconsider their ideas. Hitherto the doctrine of Free Trade had been universally accepted. The colonists were looked upon as in a state of permanent economic dependence on Britain. Their political affinities were regarded with supreme indifference. Indeed, the Benthamite idea was that the colonies were a burden on the Home Government and should be encouraged to break away. For it was seen that, although the United States had broken the political connection, she had not been less, but more, dependent economically on London since she had done so. Her indebtedness to British citizens was many times more now than it was before the War of Independence. But now that these economic dependencies of Great Britain began to use political power for the purpose of directing prices and exchange of commodities, it was seen that a new situation would have to be met. It was obvious that the industries most likely to be affected by colonial tariffs were the industries producing goods for consumption, like textile and kindred trades. The engineering and metallurgical industries were more in a position to protect themselves because they could rely on orders for the construction of railways, harbours, and public works in the colonial countries. As the industries in the colonies were mostly those of small producers of consumption goods, the British heavy and metallurgical industries did not suffer from competition and tariffs, and so they remained the only possible contractors for public works. Besides, the construction of railways in the colonies required capital, which had not yet begun to accumulate out there. So more and more did the centres of accumulated wealth for investment overseas become a dominant factor in directing the flow of trade in the products of engineering and the heavy industries. The days of Manchester were gradually passing; the days of Birmingham were coming. Free Trade was giving place to a foreign policy directed towards closed areas for concessions in undeveloped countries.

At first the effect of industrial competition on the continent of Europe and in the United States was to open out new markets for British goods and outlets for new capital investments elsewhere. It is no accident that the increase of the tendency of native capitalists to supply the needs for new capital in France, Belgium, Germany, and the United States coincided with an increase in the rate of investment of British capital in territories to which hitherto it had only gone in very small amounts. The discovery of gold in California and Australia certainly helped the process of investment of British capital in the Far West and in Australia. In India, too, in 1857, soon after the air had been cleared by the Mutiny, a veritable boom in the export of British capital for the construction of railways across that continent began. Up till then almost the only British capital in India had taken the form of investment in consumption goods for export and import and in land and estates, with houses, stores, and warehouses. But now already, by 1872, £90 millions of British capital had gone into India. Investment, indeed, to this colonial dependency was going on during these years at the rate of £6 millions a year. This was followed by big developments in Australia, South America, and Canada at the commencement of the eighties. Large capital amounts were needed by the settlers who had been drifting out there since the fifties, for the development of ranches and prairies. By 1886 £52 millions of British capital had gone into the South American republics.[1] Towards the end of the eighties British capital was going rapidly to

[1] *Export of Capital*, C. K. Hobson.

investments in Africa and the Far East. The investment in Egyptian Government loans had brought about the Egyptian crisis in the eighties and the British occupation. In China, too, there was a steady flow of capital with the gradual weakening of the financial position of the Manchu dynasty and the setting up of the Treaty Ports and the foreign concessions. Towards the end of the nineties the discovery of important mineral wealth in South Africa drew off capital supplies from London for mining developments in this quarter. In fact, more than enough new colonial areas were found during the last half of the nineteenth century to compensate for what had been lost by native accumulations replacing British capital exports to Western and Central Europe and the United States. And this was true even though by the end of the century American citizens had bought back from Europeans a hundred million dollars' worth of American railway and Government securities. British capital investments abroad were by 1900 slowing down considerably to the United States, they had practically ceased to Western and Central Europe, but they were increasing rapidly in the North American Dominion (Canada), the South American and Central American Republics, in India, the Far East, and Northern and Southern Africa.

Now if we look over the trend of British capital investments since the middle of the nineteenth century, we see a steady growth of national income derived from this source. Dr. Bowley, in his *England's Foreign Trade in the Nineteenth Century*, estimates that in 1854 £550 millions of British capital were invested abroad, partly in Government stocks and railways, and partly in railway material, manufactured goods supplied on credit, wages of engineers and workmen engaged on contractors' work abroad. In 1860 this amount had risen to £750 millions. In 1870 the inflation boom in the Franco-Prussian War still further raised the amount of foreign investment, partly by an increase in values and partly by an increased demand for war materials and for the replacement of goods destroyed by the war. In these years the amount of British capital invested abroad rose to £1,400 millions, but ten years later—in 1881—it had declined to £1,230 millions, owing to the re-establishment of normal values and a more normal demand. In 1885 it was £1,303 millions, in 1895 it was £1,600 millions, of which £500 millions were in the United States alone. Soon after the beginning of the twentieth century it had reached the £2,000 millions mark. During this time the annual income derived from this investment rose from £40 millions in 1870 to £150 millions at the end of the century. The annual export of capital over this period rose from £30 millions in 1870 to £170 millions in 1900, thus showing that during the last decades of the century the rate of export of capital annually exceeded the interest received from abroad. These years were, in fact, the peak of the boom of British economic expansion, as indicated both by the trade returns and by the figures for capital investment abroad.

At the same time it is possible to observe on examining the figures given by Dr. Bowley [1] and by C. K. Hobson [2] that there were fluctuations in the rate of capital investment over the years 1870 to 1900. The rate of foreign investments increased rapidly during the years 1870 to 1875; their rate decreased between 1875 and 1880; they increased again between 1880 and 1890 and decreased between 1890 and 1900. It would appear that there was a tendency for the

[1] *Op. cit.*   [2] *Op. cit.*

rate of capital exports to fluctuate in the following
manner:—

Increase	between	1870	and	1875
Decrease	,,	1875	,,	1880
Increase	,,	1880	,,	1890
Decrease	,,	1890	,,	1900

It is possible here to observe in three of these
periods a connection between trade boom or depression
and the condition of the capital export market. Thus
between 1875 and 1880 the general condition of
trade, as measured in exports and imports of food,
raw materials and wholly or partly manufactured
goods, was on the up grade. During this period the
rate of foreign investment abroad was declining.
From 1880 to 1890 there was a severe trade depression.
But the rate of foreign investment rose rapidly during
these years. Again, between 1890 and 1900 the depression of the eighties had given way to a steady trade
revival, but the figures for the export of capital during
these years show a distinct tendency to fall. This
seems to suggest that during the last twenty-five years,
at least, of last century the rate of flow abroad of
capital from Britain was in the inverse ratio to the
state of trade. A lack of orders of British textiles and
engineering goods in the colonial dependencies and
undeveloped areas caused new capital to keep away
from industry and to flow into foreign loans. These
may have been Government loans for the purpose of
balancing currency or loans for development schemes
under Government or private auspices for the construction of railways and other public works. It would
seem as if the capital accumulations in a big financial
centre, like London, during these years utilized a
temporary overproduction of the industrial machine
to open up new markets abroad which in another
decade would raise the demand for British goods in

these investment areas. It would, in fact, seem to suggest that the tendency was coming more and more into play, which I referred to in Chapter I, for the investment of capital abroad to be the advanced guard of, and, as it were, blazing the trail for, commerce. In other words, the granting of credit by bankers and financial development trusts to undeveloped countries went in advance of trade and was the key which opened the door to orders for the constructional industries at home and to the import of food and raw material.

On the other hand, it is worth noting that between 1870 and 1875 a different tendency was to be observed. During these years there was an increase of the rate of export of capital accompanied by a trade boom. As I have, however, noted above, these were the exceptional years of the Franco-Prussian War, when trade was booming for war purposes and when at the same time demands for capital were heavy on London as the centre of a non-combatant country. These facts would easily explain this exception to the rule which seems to be established in the case of the other decades at the end of last century. But when we come into the first decade of the twentieth century we find a similar discrepancy. Between 1900 and 1914 there was a steady increase in the rate of British capital exported abroad. At the same time, the trade returns for this period do not show sign of any depression. On the contrary, in spite of a small fluctuation in 1907 following the financial panic in America, there was a steady upward trend of trade. So that it would appear that in this period capital exports were combined with an increase in the export and import trade. But a closer examination will explain this exception. During these years a tendency was observable for the heavy industries to fall in their rate of growth. Foreign competition, particularly from the United

States and from Germany, was becoming severe in the iron, steel, and engineering trades. Hobson notes[1] on this period that among the types of industry that were declining textiles, iron, and steel could be numbered, shipbuilding and engineering showed moderate advances in the rate of production, but the rate was slower than formerly; on the other hand, chemicals, electricity, and printing showed marked advances. In other words, the foundational industries showed signs of a slowing down of the rate of increase in production, while certain specialized industries, based on new scientific discoveries in the sphere of chemistry and electricity, were forging ahead. One cannot, therefore, say that the first decade of the twentieth century indicates a boom or a depression in British industry. All one can say is that in some branches of industrial production the rate was slowing down or declining and in others going ahead. There were already indications, in fact, before the war, that the system of private capital in production and exchange was approaching a crisis in which one branch of production, hitherto dominant, was falling behind other and newer branches of production. On the one hand the rise of the new industries was tending to prevent a severe trade depression; on the other hand, the relative depression in the heavy and old basic industries was tending to force capital abroad to open out new fields in the undeveloped areas, as it did so successfully during the last decades of last century. This would account for the large increase in the rate of capital investments abroad during this time. This would also account for the great activity which was displayed in the pushing of concessions in different parts of the world. The capital that went abroad was concerned in the construction of railways, harbours,

[1] *Evolution of Modern Capitalism*, p. 388.

irrigation works, and generally of works which would provide the iron, steel, and engineering trades in England with orders for the export market. Hence the feverish activity and the drawing of State diplomacy into the hunt for concessions for the heavy industries. But unfortunately it was not only England which at this time was finding a difficulty in keeping the blast furnaces and rolling mills working. The same forces that were operating to restrict the markets of the "heavies" in England were operating also in other European countries which had started out on the race of private profit-making in constructional industries later than she had. Just as in the middle of the nineteenth century, when the United States and the Dominions were beginning to manufacture for themselves, Great Britain had to search for new markets in South America, Canada, and India, so now new outlets had to be found somewhere. But other heavy industries, besides those of Great Britain, were seeking the same.

CHAPTER IV

BRITISH CAPITAL EXPORTS ON THE EVE
OF THE WAR

IT is reported that Lord Salisbury once said that if you want to study foreign policy you must use large maps. There can be no doubt that if one inquires into the economic problems of the world on the eve of the war, more particularly concerning the movements of capital and its relation to Imperial policy, one must find some measure of geographical direction by means of which one can trace the factors at work. It is, therefore, well for us at this point to take a look at the world as it appeared on the eve of the war.

Setting aside all national, racial, or religious factors, and being guided, as we are in this inquiry, mainly by economic and social considerations, we can roughly divide up the world at this period into five principal geographical areas. The basis of the division can be made on the degree of accumulation of capital in the area or the absence of such accumulation and the rate of capital export from or import into any given area. If we take this as a means to measure our geographical boundaries, we shall be able to trace five principal areas in the world on the eve of the war. The five categories can be tabulated as follows:—

A. Old Areas of capital accumulation.
   England, Holland.

B. New Areas of capital accumulation.
   United States, France, Germany, Belgium.

C. Areas of native capital accumulation in industry, and of large undeveloped agrarian potentialities, with foreign capital invested either in Government loans or in industrial concessions.

> Canada, Argentine, Chile, parts of Brazil, Australia, South Africa, Japan, Spain, Italy, Greece.

D. Areas of native capital accumulation in local commerce and in agricultural produce with large undeveloped agrarian potentialities and with industries and public debt mainly held by foreigners.

> The Balkans, Russia, India, East Indies and Malaya, China (Treaty Ports and Concession Areas), Mexico, East Africa, Egypt, Sudan.

E. No accumulation of native capital, local industries purely handicrafts with primitive agriculture, large industry and railways almost non-existent, with Governments mortgaged to bondholders.

> Turkey, Central Asia, Persia, China (Hinterland), parts of Brazil, Central and West Africa, Syria and Mesopotamia, Indo-China.

This might, roughly speaking, be regarded as the economic position of the world in 1913. England and Holland still remained the oldest industrial countries and the largest capital exporters to the undeveloped areas in the other categories. But it was being closely followed up by those countries in Western and Central Europe and in North America in the B category, which had started out on industrial development in the last half of the nineteenth century. Particularly rapid had been the accumulations of capital in Germany and the United States, the latter after the Civil War in the sixties of last century and the former after the foundation of the Empire in the war of 1870. Both these countries had already by the commencement of this century largely dispensed with capital imports from abroad and were now beginning in their turn to export capital. We shall inquire later on into the nature, rate, and direction of the capital exports of these newer countries. France and Belgium also had dispensed

D

with capital imports and were in turn exporting. Their accumulations were older than those of the United States and Germany, and, like Britain in category A, they had built up a colonial empire for their investments. But the rate of accumulation, at least in industrial investments, was not so rapid as that of the United States and Germany, and there was a tendency in France in particular to concentrate on bond-holding capital in State loans of undeveloped countries.

In category C we have those countries which were in a much less advanced stage of industrialization, but where, nevertheless, the local inhabitants had already begun in the last decade of last century to found industries for the manufacture of their own requirements. Thus Canada could supply some at least of its own agricultural machinery by the beginning of this century, Australia part of its own textiles, South Africa part of its own engineering appliances, Japan its own steel rails and locomotives. All of those in this category had developed by the first decade of this century a considerable local production of small industrial goods, like leather goods, crockery, hardware, and of industries accessory to agriculture. All, with the possible exception of Japan and Italy, had agricultural areas, more or less considerable, which were either wholly undeveloped or only very partially developed. In both North and South America there were immense areas of ranch and prairie waiting for the settler with capital from Europe, while on the north shores of the Mediterranean were hill-sides waiting for more intensive cultivation of vine, olive, and orange. Italy and Japan fitted less easily into this category, because their undeveloped areas were not extensive and their native accumulation was fast approaching the point which made them eligible for category B. But before the war they would certainly have fitted into category C.

The countries in category D were in many respects similar to those in C. They had large agricultural areas in the tropics and temperate zones awaiting intensive cultivation. This was, and is still, the case with Russia, Mexico, and India, where cultivation of the land is primitive. In the East Indies, parts of China, East Africa, Egypt and Sudan, native land cultivation was often most intensive, but there were large areas of forest still to clear for rubber and tea plantations, deserts to irrigate for cotton, which brought these countries into the type of those which await capital investments in land and real estate by the old countries of capital accumulation. In this respect, therefore, they resembled the countries of category C. They differed, however, in the fact that they had practically no native industry. Such industries as existed were owned by foreigners. Native capital was only to be found in commerce and in the exchange of agricultural produce on the home markets with industrial goods from the foreign-owned factories. Russia was, and is, a typical instance of this. It is true, even here, native textile industries had appeared before the war, but the bulk of native capital was in commerce and it was owned by foreigners, working through native Russians to overcome legal difficulties. As, therefore, there was a large population in all these countries on land not worked to anything like its fullest extent, as there was no industry, except that which was owned by the citizens of the countries in categories A and B, it is obvious that here were fields of capital export which were of the greatest value to the countries of high capital accumulation, which were facing crises of overproduction and under-consumption at the beginning of this century in their basic and heavy industries. In addition to this type of capital export for industrial purposes there was a development of bondholder or rentier capital, of which the French peasants' investments in loans of the Tsarist Government of Russia were a typical example. A large part of this capital did not go for productive purposes at all, but for military and naval armaments and strategic railways. Much was lost in corruption of native officials and rulers. This was also the case in India in the early days of British rule there, and in Egypt in more recent times, when the British and French bondholders' money went to support profligate rulers with loans which were secured at the expense of the standard of living of the peasant population. The same could be said of China and of the interests of the international bondholders there.

In the last category, E, we come to those types of countries where there was no native industry except domestic and handicrafts, and where there was little or no accumulation of native capital even in commerce on the home market. Of course, as all through this classification, it is difficult sometimes to draw the line, and there are always a number of border-line cases which have the characteristic of more than one category. Taking it in the main, however, the countries of the Near and Middle East, Central Asia, the Hinterland of China, the vast basin of the Amazon in South America from the Atlantic to the Andes, the tropical forests of West and the upland plateaus of Central Africa, had, and still have, no native accumulations of capital at all. Exceptions to this general rule are such cases as the carpet industries of Turkey and Persia, some of which are still native, although probably the smaller part; and the native Arab accumulations in trade in native products of the African tropics across the Sahara to the shores of the Mediterranean, the native trade between Persia and Russia and between Mesopotamia and India. In the main, however, the principal exchange of tropical produce for European manufactures over these vast areas was, and is, in the hands of the countries in categories A and B. Moreover, such native Governments as still exist in these areas have been mortgaged at some time or other in the past by effete rulers to European bond-holders. Countries like Mesopotamia, Syria, Nigeria, the Gold Coast, and Indo-China are instances of countries brought more or less directly under control of categories A and B, and affording to the latter an outlet for capital investments in railways and public works, which are of no less value to the heavy industries of the old countries than those of countries in category D.

Let us now analyse in more detail the exports of capital in the A category as they appeared in the first decade of this century. We have already traced the history of Great Britain's foreign investments up to this point, and it is now advisable to see what precise changes in the direction of capital movements were going on on the eve of the Great War, in order to see what, if any, influence they may have had on the World War and the resulting economic crisis. British foreign investments were computed by Sir George Paish before the war to have reached the figure of £3,349 millions in 1910. From various sources it was possible at that time to estimate that this amount was distributed over the world in the following manner:—

	Per cent.
In the American Continent	53
In Asia	16
In Africa	14
In Australasia	12
In Europe	5

This would give us the following figures:—

In the American Continent	..	..	£1,693 millions		
In Asia	..	..	..	..	£642 ,,
In Africa	..	..	..	..	£456 ,,
In Australasia	..	..	..	..	£399 ,,
In Europe ..	..	..	..	..	£159 ,,

Let us now analyse these figures further. In 1910 the largest amount of British capital abroad was still in the United States. The families of the nobility, banks, investment trusts, generally held a portion of their capital in dollars. Particularly popular were American railways, which had for years been quoted on the London Stock Exchange. The amount of British capital in the United States in 1910 was probably slightly over £700 millions. In Canada Sir George Paish put the figure at £372 millions in that year. In Mexico an American authority has estimated British investments in that year at one-half the American, namely, £64 millions. This makes a total of £1,156 millions in Northern and Central America. If the total on the whole continent was £1,693 millions, that would leave £537 millions for investments in the Argentine, Chile, Brazil, and the other South American republics.

Coming now to Asia, Sir George Paish estimated in 1910 that British capital investments in India amounted to £365 millions. Assuming £642 millions for the whole of Asia, that would leave £247 millions for the rest of Asia. Now the Japan Year Books for 1905–1910 show £45 millions in Japanese State and municipal loans. One could allow at least £5 millions for private investments, bringing the total to £50 millions. The amount invested in the East Indies and Malaya at this time was not more than £80 millions. This leaves about £120 millions for China. In Australia British capital in 1910 was estimated at £399 millions by Sir George Paish. In Africa he estimated that in 1910

£350 millions were invested in South Africa, which left £106 millions for East and West African Crown Colonies, Egypt, Sudan, and Nigeria.

Now let us examine the position in the same countries three years later—in 1913. The *Economist* estimated £653 millions for new capital issues abroad between 1910 and 1913, which brings the total of British investments in the colonies, dominions, and foreign countries in 1913 to £3,972 millions. Taking now the American continent, we find we can roughly piece together what had happened in the three intervening years. In Mexico in 1913 British investments were estimated at about £100 millions, an increase of £36 millions.[1] In Canada in 1913 British investments were estimated at £376 millions, an increase of £4 millions.[2] In the United States British investments are estimated in 1913 by Sir George Paish at £754 millions, an increase of £34 millions over 1910.[3] As regards South America, Brazilian figures in 1923 estimated British investments in Brazil on the eve of the war at £238 millions. In the rest of South America in 1913 they were estimated at £477 millions.[4] This made an increase over the whole of South America in three years of the enormous figure of £715 millions, showing clearly the new direction of British overseas capital movements.

In Asia a considerable flow of capital from England was taking place to India. In India in 1913 the public debt held by England was £152 millions; the joint-stock companies operating in India and registered in London had a capital of £192 millions, those registered in India £150 millions, of which probably about

---

[1] *The Times*, quoting United States Department of Commerce.
[2] J. Connor, in Canadian *Forward* (Toronto).
[3] *Encyclopædia Britannica*, Supplement, p. 519.
[4] *American Federal Reserve Bulletin.*

£100 millions was held by British citizens. This would mean that about £450 millions was the amount held by Great Britain in India. In the rest of Asia British capital in China was: in Government bonds £25 millions, railways £15 millions.[1] In addition to this there was over £160 millions invested in various transport undertakings, shipping, and general industries in China. This makes a total of a little over £200 millions for all China. In Japan Government loans, municipal and bank shares issued and quoted in London amount to £70 millions.[2] In the East Indies and Straits Settlements it is probable that on the eve of the war about £120 millions were invested in public works and rubber plantations, of which rubber investments had absorbed about £20 millions. In the Philippines British investments in 1913 were about £40 millions.

In Australia fresh capital raised in London between 1910 and 1913 amounted to £37 millions, making a total of £436 millions. In Africa about £30 millions of British capital seems to have gone between 1910 and 1913, according to contemporary Stock Exchange reports both in London and in Cape Town, into Government loans, public works, land development, mines, and railways. This includes also Rhodesia and the Portuguese colonies. In Egypt, the Sudan, and the British East and West African Crown Colonies the public debt and railway investments in 1913 in sterling amounted to about £150 millions.

In Europe a total British investment in 1913 amounted to £184 millions, but of this £103 millions were in Russia (£53 millions in State loans and £50 millions in industries).[3]

---

[1] *China Year Book*, 1925, and *Financial News*, December 9, 1926.
[2] *Japan Year Book* and *Stock Exchange Year Book*.
[3] *Russian Debts and Russian Reconstruction*, Moulton and Pasvolsky. N.Y., pp. 21 and 22.

BRITISH FOREIGN INVESTMENTS (*in million £*).

	1910.	1913.	Increase over 1910.	Priority of Increase.
AMERICAN CONTINENT—				
Mexico	64	100	+ 36	7
Canada	372	376	+ 4	12
United States	720	754	+ 34	8
Argentine, Chile, Brazil, and other S. American Republics	537	715	+ 178	1
	1,693	1,945		
ASIATIC CONTINENT—				
India	365	450	+ 85	3
China	120	208	+ 88	2
East Indies and Straits Settlements, Malaya, etc.	80	120	+ 40	5
Japan	50	70	+ 20	10
Philippines	27	40	+ 13	11
	642	888		
AUSTRALASIA	399	436	+ 37	6
AFRICAN CONTINENT—				
South Africa	350	380		
Rest of Africa, with Egypt and Sudan	106	150	+ 74	4
	456	530		
EUROPE	159			
Russia		103		
Rest of Europe		81	+ 25	9
		184		
Total	£3,349	£3,983	£634	

We thus see that the increases of British capital investments in foreign countries take the following order:—

1. Argentine, Brazil, Chile, and other South American Republics.
2. China.
3. India.
4. South Africa and African Crown Colonies, Egypt and Sudan.
5. East Indies and Malaya.
6. Australia.
7. Mexico.
8. United States.
9. Europe.
10. Japan.
11. Philippines.
12. Canada.

It is obvious from this list that the flow of British capital before the war was going more and more to develop those areas in the C, D, and E categories in South America, Africa, and Southern and Eastern Asia. It was almost stagnant in the North American continent, and increasing at a slower rate than formerly in the East of Europe. It was clear also that the chief spheres of interest now were Argentine, the Far East, South Africa, India, and the African Crown Colonies with Egypt and the Sudan. But events were happening in the rest of Europe. Other countries in the B category had eyes on some of these last areas for capital investment, or at least were economically penetrating regions which bordered on them. Here we come up against a most important factor in immediate pre-war history, and it behoves us, therefore, to investigate the nature of the conflicting interests which arose from the economic penetration of capital from the A and B categories of countries.

CHAPTER V

GROWTH OF CAPITAL EXPORT IN NEW AREAS OF ACCUMULATION: FRANCE AND GERMANY

It will be remembered that in our geographical division of the world on the basis of capital accumulation the second or B category includes the United States, France, Germany, and Belgium. We have seen in former chapters that throughout the latter half of the nineteenth century the United States was gradually emancipating itself from economic dependence for capital supplies on Europe, till by the beginning of this century it was embarking upon a career of capital export on its own with its consequent Imperialistic foreign policy. The ground had been largely cleared for this development by the Civil War. This gave the northern industrial States control over the cheap black labour of the South by breaking the southern cotton planters' monopoly over the labour market, of which the principal feature was the institution of slavery. Other countries on the European continent were also ceasing to be dependent on Great Britain and Holland, these two countries of the oldest mercantile capital. France had been the first to walk the road of financial independence. After the reconstruction loans financed by London through Rothschild and Baring which set her on her feet after the disasters of the Napoleonic wars, she became a land of peasant investors, who converted the gold and silver savings in their stockings into foreign Government loans. In spite of further revolutionary movements which set up and upset again a "Citizen King" and a Republic, this process of rentier accumulation went on apace. By 1830 France could borrow on almost as good terms as the British Government could from the international Jewish houses in Frankfurt or from the old-established London City firms. She had only to offer 1 per cent. more than British Government loans and the money was there. After 1850 French industrial development, with the aid of British capital, began and lasted through the era of railway construction. While the Englishman, Thomas Brassey, was building her railways, the French peasants were accumulating the savings of their husbandry. This national investment fund, which had begun during the reign of the "Citizen King" in the thirties, grew, till by 1850 France was lending capital abroad at the same time as she was importing it for industrial construction from England. By 1870, when the flow from England had all but ceased, she had become a capital-exporting country, and her total foreign investments in that year amounted to between £5 and £6 millions sterling. The direction of these investments was mainly towards the basin of the Mediterranean and towards the shores of the Caribbean Sea. She was financing the Government of Spain, the Khedive of Egypt with an eye upon the Suez Canal, the Governments in Mexico and Brazil. She was starting on her career as the financier of Governments, as the holder of bonds and first charges on national assets with all the political influence which this brings in its train. Towards the end of last century she was also exporting industrial goods and industrial capital, more particularly to North Africa, the Near East, and Russia. But her expansion as an exporter of industrial capital was not as rapid as her expansion as an exporter of mortgage capital. She tended to develop the sleeping-partner type of investment which would always carry with it the right to foreclose and become the possessor of the national assets or the virtual controller of the Colonial Government.

Possibly France's history in this connection was influenced by the course of the Franco-Prussian War. The loss of the iron-bearing strata in Lorraine under the Peace of Frankfurt gave industrial supremacy on the Continent to her powerful and now united rival in the North. Up till this time Germany had no large industrial prospects. Up till the middle of the nineteenth century she had retained much of her mediæval feudalism. The country was intersected by the estates of petty princes and grand-dukes, each with its own customs and hindrances to national, let alone international, trade. The power of the agrarian nobility was supreme over the administrations and there was little more than language and culture to mark national unity. The revolution of 1848 prepared the way for the modern capitalistic State, but prior to this, and perhaps to some extent causing it, was the growth of railways, which, with the aid of Dutch, English, and Rhineland Jewish capital, had been slowly creeping over the surface of the North-German plain. The German mediæval back-garden was beginning to flower with the plants of modern industrialism. Then followed in quick succession the creation of the Zollverein or Customs Union of Germany, the establishment of a modern banking system, enabling the national savings to be accumulated and invested first at home and then abroad, the big industrial discoveries with the aid of German scientists, the new processes of smelting steel, the political union of the country at Versailles, and last, but not least, the annexation of Lorraine, which provided, although this was not known at the time to the Prussian generals who dictated the peace, the raw material of the great Westphalian heavy industries. The extraordinary mushroom-growth of modern

Germany was mainly developed on its industrial side. Germany does not appear upon the scene during the nineteenth century at any time as an exporter of capital to foreign Governments. The German investing public have been concerned first with developing their own country industrially and with exporting manufactured goods and commodities. What export of capital there had been was mainly industrial, to provide equipment to the industries of neighbouring countries in Eastern Europe, the Balkans, and the Near East. The German Government found outlets for the activities of its teeming urban population and for the accumulation of public savings, more by the construction of railways in the Near East than by lending money to decadent Governments with a view to acquiring political influence, as the French did.

Thus by the commencement of this century Germany and France and, linked economically with both of them, Belgium, were the typical representatives of the B category of countries of new capital accumulation in Europe. Their industrial development had been much later than that of Britain. In 1909 the total capital invested in joint-stock companies in Britain was £2,160 millions, in Germany only £390 millions. In France the only figure available is for 1898, where £540 millions, including railway investments, compares with about £2,000 millions in Great Britain at that time.[1] But if the difference in the state of industrialization between countries in categories A and B in Europe on the eve of the Great War were great, the difference in the rate of accumulation of capital was still greater. Thus we find that between 1870 and 1914 the amount of foreign investments had increased five times in France and only two and a quarter times in Great

[1] *Economic Development of France and Germany*, by J. H. Clapham, p. 400.

Britain. Between 1902 and 1914 it had increased twelve times in Germany, while it had only added 30 per cent. to its value during this period in Great Britain.

This rapid rise in the rate of accumulation of capital savings in these newer industrial countries raised at once the question of the export of the surplus to new investment areas, for French and German bankers were now finding remunerative rates outside their own countries. Investment at home still went on, and indeed increased in rate, and the development of the nation's resources and industrial equipment continued, but a portion of the new accumulations wandered out to earn higher rates elsewhere.

Now this search for investment areas on the part of new economic units in the world necessarily disturbed the international equilibrium existing during the greater part of the nineteenth century, when Great Britain was the only large exporter of capital, with Holland following on a smaller scale. But already during the nineties of last century the United States was beginning to buy back much of the railway stock taken up originally by European lenders, and soon was pushing its capital investments into new industrial enterprises in Canada. This was followed by a big drive towards the Caribbean Sea and the South American Republics. I will not delay here by entering into any details about the competition between this section of the B category of countries with the A category. For the race for foreign investment areas between Great Britain and the United States in South America, though keen, has not, as yet, brought with it those political repercussions which have led to grave international crises. There has never been any threat of war between these two countries because of American economic penetration of Canada. This is partly, no doubt, due to the geographical proximity of Canada and the United States and to the large undefended land frontier which leaves military preponderance so entirely on one side. Secondly, there can be little doubt that the interlocking of many interests in Wall Street and the City tends to dull the edge of competition to some extent. Most big investment houses or financial administrators of accumulated funds in England place a portion of their investments in dollar securities. Many titled families have either by marriage or by investment got some holdings across the Atlantic. Moreover, the tie of common language and the existence of a form of society which gives social prestige to the moneyed interests rather than to landed or to semi-feudal military castes, removes other causes for conflict. Since the Civil War and the victory of Northern dollars over Southern chattel slavery the great Republic and the Island Monarchy have much the same economic framework. Capital could flow easily between the two. Intercourse was free and intermarriage frequent.

This could not be said of the relations between Great Britain and the other countries on the Continent, and this introduced a new non-economic factor. France and Germany, for instance, had certain linguistic and social characteristics which made a ready flow of capital between them and Great Britain more difficult than between the latter and the United States. The difficulty was all the greater in the case of Germany, where the remains of an older pre-capitalistic economy existed with great persistency until quite recent years. It is best explained by reference to the fact that in Germany all the higher posts of the civil and diplomatic service, Army and Navy, were reserved for the landed nobility. This gave the latter a certain privilege over pure financial interests and militated against a flow of capital between Germany and countries where financial and industrial interests had paramount influence over the Government. More than that, it exaggerated possible points of friction where German capital competed with capital of other countries of the A category and even of those of the B category. Barring an Anglo-German loan in China in the nineties, there were no colonial enterprises promoted jointly by financiers of these two countries. The attempts to co-operate in the Near East failed, as we shall see presently. Again, while some German capital had gone to the New World early in this century and was converted into United States railway securities and bonds or was assisting in the development of Canada, there was little return flow of American capital into Germany. There was little joint participation of German and American capital in industrial undertakings in Europe. There were only agreements between German industrial "Cartels" and British and American companies for the regulation of prices. And this was only in the initial stages. Herr Stresemann in this connection made an interesting statement to a gathering of business men in Dresden in November 1926, in which he is reported to have said that it was a great mistake for Germany before the war to have excluded so drastically foreign capital. He ascribed this policy to a mistaken sense of pride, and expressed the belief that Germany might have secured with foreign capital, if not allies, at least neighbours with an interest in her fate. The sense of pride to which Herr Stresemann referred here was the policy of the Junkers and of the captains of heavy industry, whose families were often inter-married, in developing their national heritage without the assistance of the international money market. It was notorious, of course, that pre-war Prussia

E

had been for generations the home of anti-Semitism and the accomplice of Tsarist Russia in anti-Jewish measures. This naturally estranged the Hohenzollern regime from at least one powerful section of the inter- national money-lending houses. The Rothschilds and the Rhineland bankers were tolerated, but that was all. A story is told that a Rothschild once got the ear of the Kaiser and a promise that his son should receive a commission in the Prussian Guards. When this came to the ears of the Junker entourage of the Court, the Kaiser was constrained by very strong pressure to go back on his promise. This little story shows which way the wind blew in pre-war Germany. Sheltered by Bismarck's high tariffs, which protected agrarian produce, iron, steel, and the manufactured articles of heavy industry, the Junkers and their industrialist friends were secured in their home markets and invested the proceeds of their capital accumulations in railway enterprises abroad. The German finishing industries, textiles, general com- merce, and banking, had no very large say in German Government policy. Where German banks, like the Deutsche Bank, financed such enterprises as the Bagdad Railway, the controlling influence was not Rhineland finance, but Junkers, Westphalian heavy industry, and persons in touch with the Govern- ment departments, who were well represented on the directorate. Nor was Berlin at this time a financial centre for the attraction of investors in securities outside Germany. The list of shares quoted on the Berlin Stock Exchange did not include many of the prominent securities of international reputation which were always a feature of the London Exchange, and to a lesser extent of Paris. Only on one occasion before the war did the German banks bring in foreign assistance. When the Junker-heavy industry alliance in

1911 was in conflict with French financial interests in Morocco over the future concessions and opportunities for investment in that country, a serious financial crisis swept over Germany. The prospect of war found the German banking system isolated from the big Jewish, British, and American banking groups and quite unprepared for such a situation. There was a run on the banks, which required 300 million marks to save themselves. Accommodation was provided by American banks, "who saw their opportunity and lent at the rate of 6 per cent. and 7 per cent., which in normal times Berlin could have got for 3 per cent. and 4 per cent." [1]

Thus we see that of all the new countries of capital accumulation Germany was the one which was the most isolated from the rest. Capital accumulation was going on on purely national lines and under the influence of a Government which had semi-feudal characteristics. Thus the psychical groundwork for friction was prepared at points where German foreign investments impinged on the rights of similar investments in A and other B category countries. It will be our next step to consider where the points of impingement were.

[1] Fullerton, *Problems of Power.*

CHAPTER VI

FRENCH AND GERMAN FOREIGN INVESTMENTS AND THEIR AREAS OF IMPINGEMENT

IN 1914 the total amount of foreign investments of the French Republic was estimated at about £1,600 millions.[1] It is, however, not easy to get a clear idea of the area of the distribution of these investments. In some countries it is possible to know the amount of French capital invested fairly accurately. But in others it must of necessity be of the nature of guess-work, and can only be surmised by a process of elimination of other known factors. In their book on *Russian Debts and Russian Reconstruction*, Pasvolsky and Moulton give the total amount of French capital in Russia as £408 millions, of which £308 millions were in the pre-war State Debt, £40 millions in the new War Debt, and £60 millions in industrial securities. In the area of the colonial world France was clearly a bondholder more than a holder of industrial concessions. In Turkey the amount of French capital in 1914 was given in Earle's *Turkey, the Great Powers and the Bagdad Railway*, at £500 millions. This amount consisted for the greater part of holdings in the Imperial Ottoman Debt, which again indicated that in this part of the East also France was the bond-holder more than the industrial *entrepreneur*. I do not know of any exact figures for the French investments in Egypt, but they could hardly have been less than £50 millions before the war, and were partly in State Bonds and partly in trading enterprises. In North Africa the amount of Moroccan Public Debt

Hon. George Peel, *Public Finance of France.*

held in France in 1914 was £3 millions, while French industrial capital there was probably about £10 millions and in other parts of the South Mediterranean seaboard another £10 millions, making a total of £23 millions. In the other African Protectorates and in French Indo-China, French investments are given in the *Encyclopædia Britannica* at £120 millions in 1905. This would probably make them nearer £150 millions by 1914. In the Balkans, French capital took the form of railway investments and commercial enterprises, and amounted to about £150 millions. £50 millions were invested in Austria-Hungary before the war largely in bonds, and a little over £20 millions were in Germany in the form of mining companies and participation shares in German industrial enterprises. In China, according to the *China Year Book*, £17 millions French capital in 1914 were in railways, £8 millions in banks, and £13 millions in Government loans. In Japan, Government loans subscribed in France in 1914 amounted to some £22 millions. This makes a total foreign investment so far accounted for of £1,380 millions. This leaves a balance to make up the total of £1,600 millions of roughly £220 millions. This could reasonably be taken to represent capital invested in the American continent, the United States, Canada, and the South and Central American republics.

Coming now to Germany, Mr. J. M. Keynes [1] gives the total German foreign investments before the war at between £1,000 and £1,250 millions. Of this, Keynes, quoting a census of the Austrian Ministry of Finance in 1912, puts the German investments in Austria-Hungary at £197 millions. As regards Russia, he puts German capital in commercial and industrial enterprises at £95 millions and quotes Sartorius von Waltershausen to show that her investments in Russian

Economic Consequences of the Peace, p. 162.

Government securities amounted to £150 millions in 1906, giving a total capital in Russia of £245 millions. On the other hand, Pasvolsky and Moulton [1] put German capital in Russia at only £32 millions for commercial and industrial enterprises before the war, and as regards Government Bonds say that 80 per cent. was held in France and 14 per cent. in Great Britain, which, with a total State Debt in 1913 of £3,850 millions, leaves less than £20 millions for the rest of the world. So, according to this, German capital in Russian State Bonds could not have been more than £10 millions, if as much. The evidence of these two authorities is conflicting, but it is probable that Germany confined herself mainly to commercial and industrial enterprises in Russia, but probably had between £50 and £100 millions in that country. In Turkey, also, Germany was little interested in the Ottoman Public Debt. Her interest was mainly in the Bagdad Railway, of which 20 per cent. of the shares were offered on the Berlin Bourse.[2] In all, Germany seems to have sunk about £100 millions in railway enterprises in Turkey. This brings the total of German investments in the three chief countries of the Near East—Austria, Russia, and Turkey—to a little under £400 millions. Coming to colonial investments in Africa and the Far East, in China £3 million Government Bonds and £3 million railway bonds were held,[4] and another £5 millions in industry. In North Africa, mainly Morocco, Germany held about £20 millions invested in mines and industries, according to statements in the German Press at the time of the Morocco crisis. In the German African

[1] *Russian Debts and Russian Reconstruction*, McGraw Hill Book Co. N.Y., 1924, p. 21.
[2] *Le Chemin de fer de Bagdad au point de vue Politique, Economique et Financier*, by Alexandre Ilitsch. Paris, 1913.
[3] *China Year Book.*

colonies £25 millions were invested in railway construction in 1912.[1] Another £10 millions would account
for all that was put into other enterprises in the
German colonies. This brings the total German
investments in Eastern Europe, the Near East, Far
East, and Africa to about £470 millions, which leaves
a balance of roughly £600 millions for the rest of
the world. According to a German authority,[2] German
securities in Italy, Spain, United States, and South
America amounted in 1913 to an equivalent of £300
millions, which would leave a balance of £300 millions
in England, France, and Belgium.

These figures are very largely guesswork, but two
facts seem to come from them. Firstly, on the eve
of the war the German banks and financial and
industrial houses had actually got as much as £300
millions in England, France, and Belgium in the way
of long or short term loans and industrial investments.
This is a remarkable indication that the business
world of Germany was not only not planning the
war, but, under the influence of the economic and
political agreements with England over Africa and
the Near East, did not appear to regard such an
event as even remotely probable. Otherwise common
prudence would have suggested that they should reduce
something of their £300 millions holdings in England,
France, and Belgium. For, as it turned out, the
greater part of this capital was forfeited at the outbreak of war and sequestered as "enemy property."
Secondly, it is clear that Germany, like France,
had quite an appreciable sum invested in America,
but, as in the case of British capital in that continent,
its political significance was slight. It is true that the

[1] *Deutschlands Kolonialpolitik*, Hagen. Berlin, 1913.
[2] *Die deutsche Banken im Ausland*, Karl Sreasser, Emil Reinhardt.
Munich. 1925.

factor of common language and culture, making joint industrial enterprises with citizens of the United States possible, did not apply in the case of French and German capital operating across the Atlantic. But on the other hand the relatively small amounts there and the political and strategic advantages of the United States over all Europeans prevented the investment fields of the New World from being an area of friction between France and Germany. Foreign capital was welcome in the United States, but its owners could not treat North America as they treated the investment fields of the Near East.

On the other hand, the situation was very different along the shores of the Mediterranean, beyond the Carpathian Mountains and across the Dardanelles. Here still unspent animosities between European countries from pre-capitalistic days combined with the rivalry engendered by the ceaseless export of capital for investment in modern times to create an atmosphere in which the economic conflict might more easily be solved by an appeal to the sword. It is no accident, indeed, that the two international crises which in one case nearly did, and in the other actually did, lead to war, arose in territories bordering the Mediterranean and lying in close proximity to the straits dividing Europe from Asia. It has been sometimes said that the European War nearly broke out over Morocco three years earlier than it actually did. It is an interesting, but futile, speculation whether war might have broken out over the Agadir incident in 1911 if certain leading personalities in England and Germany had chanced to behave rather more foolishly and ill-temperedly than they actually did. On the whole, however, there are two factors which seem to point to the fact that the situation was not yet ripe for Armageddon. Firstly, the capital sums involved in

North Africa were not sufficiently large to make a conflagration very likely without some other over-riding factor. Thus we have seen that France was interested in those territories only to the amount of £23 millions and Germany to the amount of only £15 millions. The firm of Mannesmann of Düsseldorf were the chief interested partners in mining conces-sions on the German side, and they were not popular with governing circles in Berlin or with the powerful armament firm of Krupps. Other factors, moreover, were not present. The crisis revealed the German Reich in a weak position financially. The economic fabric of pan-German agrarian-Junker and heavy industry exhibited glaring fissures, which could not be plastered over in a hurry. The panic on the Berlin Bourse during the Morocco crisis of that year was only prevented from developing into something more serious by the intervention of the American banks.

It was on the Eastern side of the Mediterranean that the more serious danger of a conflagration breaking out existed. Ever since the occupation of Egypt, British influence in Constantinople had been gradually on the decline. German influence, on the other hand, had been as steadily rising. The export of French, German, and British capital to Asiatic Turkey for the construction of railways had been going on since 1888 in more or less equal proportions. But in 1903 the grant by the Sultan of the concession for the construction of the Bagdad Railway to a German concern indicated that the German Reich had won the chief influence over the decaying native Govern-ment of Turkey. The import and export trade between Turkey and Germany between 1900 and 1910 rose 166 per cent., while that between Turkey and France rose only 17 per cent. and between Britain and Turkey 25 per cent. But the weak financial position of Germany was seen from the fact that its bankers did not feel confident of being able to finance the Bagdad Railway without outside assistance. From the outset they offered British and French capital one-third each of the shares. An agreement had already been made in 1899 between French banks and the Deutsche Bank for the joint financing of smaller railway schemes in Turkey, and at first the French Government declared its readiness to let the agreement apply for the financing of the Bagdad Railway. But the whole idea awoke the bitter antagonism of the Conservative Government in Great Britain. The big shipping interests feared the loss of freights and mails on the overland route to the East from Berlin to the Persian Gulf. The British heavy industries were up in arms for fear that the control of the orders for rails, locomotives, and rolling stock would be left in German hands. The Anglo-Indian and naval and military bureaucracy in Whitehall feared the appearance of a new military alliance between Germany and Turkey. British pressure was put on France, and the French Bourse was closed to Bagdad Railway issues. Nevertheless even then a large block of Bagdad Railway shares were held in France. Meanwhile the Turkish Government sought to smooth over the growing antagonisms of the Imperial Powers by proposing a scheme for financing the railway which would have led to the taking up of 20 per cent. of the shares in all four countries—France, Germany, Britain, and Turkey. This proposal for the internationalization of the undertaking was rejected by the Liberal Government of Mr. Asquith on the ground that it would involve an increase of the Turkish customs as guarantee for the loans. Then just as things looked at their worst, there came one of those curious changes in the political atmosphere, like a burst of sunshine amid April storms. Towards the end of 1913 there was a sudden move for a Franco-German economic understanding over Asiatic Turkey. The French group interested in railway construction in Asiatic Turkey agreed with the German Bagdad Railway and the Deutsche Bank upon spheres of operation in those territories. Northern Anatolia and the Armenian vilayets were to be the sphere of the French concessionaires, Central Anatolia was to be the German sphere; railways in these two spheres were to be linked up on completion and new works at the port of Heraclea on the Black Sea were to be joint Franco-German enterprises. Syria was to be regarded as a French sphere for railways and the Deutsche Bank was to buy up the 70 million franc shares of the Imperial Ottoman Bank in the Bagdad Railway.

This sudden *volte-face* of the French concession interests caused alarm in London. But the effect was to induce some of the financial groups there to incline also towards an economic *rapprochement* with similar groups in Germany, for fear of losing any share of the bear's skin. There were two or three special groups in London which were concerned in this new move. First there were a few people interested in Mesopotamian irrigation schemes, for whom an agreement with Germany, marking out spheres of exploitation, would be of advantage. For these it was arranged that Mesopotamia was to be an English sphere and the plains of Cilicia a German sphere for all matters concerning irrigation. Secondly, there were the oil interests. For these the Turkish Petroleum Company was formed in March 1914, in which the National Bank of Turkey, controlled by Sir Ernest Cassel and Lord Inchcape, held 50 per cent. of the shares, the Royal Dutch Shell 25 per cent., and the Deutsche Bank 25 per cent. of the shares. This gave

German interests a share in the oil exploitation of Mesopotamia, leaving the control, however, British. Then there were the British shipping interests on the Tigris, and bound up with them the Manchester cotton piece goods trade from England via the Gulf to Persia. These were satisfied with an arrangement to regard the shipping on the Tigris as a British sphere, to secure that no discriminatory tariffs were levied on German railways in Mesopotamia and that the German railway should not come beyond Basra, leaving the Gulf section to be constructed by British groups. The British Government, like all Governments, influenced in policy by those who were temporarily in the ascendancy, gave a political seal to this economic agreement in June 1914. In Africa, too, economic and political co-operation between England and Germany had now become the order of the day. In 1914, on the eve of the war, a draft treaty between England and Germany was initialled under which an Anglo-German loan was to be granted to Portugal on security of the colonial customs and providing for the eventual partition of the Portuguese colonies. The pacific Manchester School had got the ear of Sir Edward Grey and had made the most of it. That, however, did not close that strange chapter in the immediate pre-war relations of the great capital-exporting Powers. A section of the capital exporters in each of these countries had reached an agreement. It almost seemed as if the sword which had threatened since the Morocco crisis would rust in its sheath and that capital investments would flow once more from the exporting centres in Europe by agreement into appointed spheres. Such a solution was certainly very nearly being reached over the most hotly contested area even on the eve of Armageddon. This fact certainly does not support the view that the

existence of two competing Imperial Powers vitally
interested in foreign investment must of necessity
lead to war. In this case there were powerful capitalist
forces, comprising railway interests, oil, cotton, irrigation capital, and some shipping which had actually
made an agreement, and this would probably have lasted
many years. But there were clearly a number of other
factors at work. First of all there were elements both
in Britain and France which could not be reconciled
to a German trunk route across the Ottoman Empire.
That vast aggregate of British industrial shipping and
commercial interests of all kinds invested in India
feared the proximity of a new competitor, and would
not accept without a struggle anything less than the
position of dominant partner. The loss of Asia Minor
as an area for the export of steel rails and rolling stock
on credit, to be paid for by kilometric guarantee
over a term of years, rankled in the minds of heavy
industries of the Midlands and the North-East Coast
of England, as it did with the iron and steel masters
of the industrial areas of Northern France. The latter
also had set covetous eyes for some years past on the
great iron deposits of the Saar and Lorraine, and saw
in the conflict an occasion to reopen the struggle for
the unification of the mineral resources of the Rhine
Valley under Latin hegemony. Then there were the
naval and military interests in both England, France,
and Germany, whose machinery, naval programmes,
conscript armies, and missions to Turkey had been
built up on the assumption that economic rivalry would
lead to a conflict and who were always anxious for
any excuse to use what they had so laboriously created
and now handled with pride. But these were, I think,
at least as regards the three Western Powers, subordinate to the economic interests. By themselves they
could not have made the war, but, given an unstable

equilibrium between pacific and bellicose capitalistic interests in two groups of nations, the conditions were favourable for the more decisive influence of the naval and military bureaucracy, who otherwise would be held subordinate to the industrialist, trader, and financier. Under these conditions great modern wars are germinated, as the World War was in August 1914. That war was an incidental event in the economic rivalry of capital-exporting Powers. It was an outcome of that rivalry, but it was not necessarily the logical consequence of that rivalry. The acute phase of this crisis over the concessions in the East between England, France, and Germany might easily have passed and given way to international agreement. But the long continuation of an uncertain balance made the rivalry between the European Powers in the Near and Middle East a much more dangerous matter than the rivalry between the European Powers singly and the United States in Central and Southern America, where, through the predominance of one side, the balance was so much less even. It was the uncertain balance in Asia that allowed the element of chance in human affairs to come into play. This in turn gave undue influence to two factors—the military and naval machines of the Great Powers of the West and the governmental systems and social institutions in Eastern Europe which had their origin in pre-capitalistic civilization.

CHAPTER VII

RUSSO-AUSTRIAN CÆSARISM IN EASTERN EUROPE

IT is to the semi-feudal society in the old Austrian
and Russian Empires that we have to turn to find the
principal key which unlocked the kennels of the Dogs
of War in 1914. For in spite of the Anglo-German
agreements on Mesopotamia and Africa, in spite of
the Franco-German agreement on Asia Minor railways, in spite of the lukewarmness and finally the
direct opposition of the German Government to the
Austrian adventure in Serbia, it was still possible for
the murder of an Archduke to set the military machine
of the Austrian War Office going on July 29, 1914.
That act of the semi-feudal, irresponsible militarists
on the Eastern marches of Europe overrode the
arrangements of the pacifically inclined financiers and
company promoters in Paris, London, and Berlin, and
of the three Foreign Offices, and strengthened the
irreconcilable industrialists and certain shipping interests in England, France, and Germany, as well
as the military and naval machines there. And so,
too, the provocative Russian general mobilization on
the German front on July 30, 1914, which made
war inevitable, was another of those irresponsible acts
of a feudal agrarian and military caste, the social
pillars of the Russian Autocracy, to ward off the
threatened revolution by adventures in a foreign war,
which, if successful, would bring with it governorships and administrative posts in Constantinople and
in the territories conquered from Asiatic Turkey.
The Government of Russia, in fact, was of such a
kind as to break through the calculations of the

Chancelleries and of high finance in Western Europe. For Russia was at this time in a transition state. She was gradually passing out of her isolated feudal past. She had now over 50,000 miles of railways. Her output of iron ore had quadrupled in ten years and her textile output had trebled in the same time. The industrial revolution was beginning. Foreign capitalists were engaged in working her mineral resources, native Russian employers had built factories and were supplying the home market with perishable goods, textiles, hardware, etc., for local consumption. They were even pushing their wares out across the Eastern frontiers to the Turkish, Persian, Central Asian, and Chinese markets. A small but increasing export of Moscow manufactures was competing with the goods from Western Europe in the years before the war. Thus there was a class of Russian merchant and manufacturer of articles of general consumption who was interested in Imperial expansion in Asia for commercial reasons. Russia was becoming a country of mercantile capitalism in loose alliance, at least as far as foreign policy was concerned, with the feudal nobility. The former sought markets for Moscow textiles, the latter administrative posts in the East. The Russian heavy industries, being almost entirely owned by foreigners and having an unlimited home market, had not started out on the path of Imperial expansion. Russian Imperialism was thus a very different type from the Imperialism of Great Britain, France, and Germany. It did not seek either foreign markets for steel rails and other products of heavy industry, nor did it seek investments for capital. It sought, like Manchester merchants sought eighty years ago, markets for perishable goods and, as it had to meet competition, it sought the aid of tariffs and military pressure on weaker Oriental neighbours,

like Turkey and Persia, to secure those markets.
But side by side with this there was a desire to prevent
the economic development of these Asiatic regions.
The primitive mercantile capital of Russia wanted
these countries to remain in a condition to receive
its goods, which were often carried long journeys by
camel. It did not want railways and harbours built,
for these would link these countries more with the
West and loosen the economic ties to Russia. It
opposed West European finance capital which was
seeking to build railways and open up Asia Minor
and Persia. But being unable to prevent altogether
the expansion of European finance across these regions,
it strove to confine it to certain areas away from the
borders of the Empire, keeping other areas as its own
preserve, which it might develop or hold back as it
desired. Russian policy in Asia Minor concentrated
upon three points: (1) the advancement of Russian
general trade by obtaining control over an ice-free
sea, either in the Persian Gulf or on the Gulf of
Alexandretta; (2) the desire to retard the development of Turkey and particularly that part of it bordering on Russia; (3) the desire to have a free hand to
interfere in the internal affairs of Persia.[1] There were
thus two main motives behind Russian Imperialism—
expansion with a view to administrative posts for the
Tsarist nobility and bureaucracy, and the retaining of
markets for perishable wares by retarding the growth
of the higher forms of capitalist economy, which
were spreading into Asia from Western Europe.
Russian Imperialism was from a capitalistic standpoint backward and reactionary. In this connection a
very interesting passage can be read in the com-
munications between the Russian Ambassador in

[1] *Le Chemin de fer de Bagdad,* by A. Ilitsch. Misch & Thron,
Paris, 1913, p. 100.

F

Constantinople and the Russian Foreign Minister in February 1912. It was just before the Franco-German understanding on railway construction in Asia Minor. The Tsarist Government, fearing that an agreement between these two Western Powers might lead to the economic development of Turkey, might prevent her break-up, and might damage the market for Russian textiles, was moving in Europe to prevent an agreement. A syndicate of French financiers was preparing a plan for the construction of railways running from Samsun to Sivas, Erzinjan, Trebizond, Erzerum, and Diabekr, to connect up with the German Bagdad Railway on the one side and with the Russian railway system on the other. Commenting upon the coming report of the French engineers, the Russian Ambassador in Constantinople reports to his chief: "It seems to me necessary to influence the French concessionaires, for it would be advantageous for us if the French engineers reported unfavourably on the projected railways, especially on those which are inimical to us. In this connection we may stress the fact that the line Trebizond-Erzerum has enormous technical difficulties."[1] Here we have a picture of Tsarist diplomacy, unable to hinder the expansion of West European heavy industries and of the financial groups behind them into Asiatic countries but trying to harness them to its policy.

Sometimes Tsarist diplomacy, in order to obstruct the extension of railways which would open up the Near and Middle East to the heavy industries and finance of the West, would propose fantastic counter-schemes. To this category would belong the proposal

---

[1] *Diplomatische Aktenstuecke zur Geschichte der Ententepolitik der Vorkriegsjahre*, edited by B. von Siebert, former Secretary of the Imperial Russian Embassy in London. Pub. Gruyter, Berlin and Leipzig, 1921.

for a Danube-Adriatic railway across the mountains of Serbia and Montenegro. Its commercial value could only be nil, but its diplomatic value was to strike across the Austrian proposal of 1908 to construct a line from the end of the Bosnian railway through Mitrovitza in the Sanjak of Novibazar to the Ægean Sea. Both these proposals were, in fact, fantastic, and served the military interests of the semi-feudal monarchies of Russia and Austria rather than of the financiers of London, Berlin, and Paris. An even better example was seen in 1912, when the serious and highly practicable British proposal for the construction of a railway in South Persia from Khoramabad to Mohammerah, connecting the Gulf with Central Persia in the interests of trade with the West, was countered by the Russian Government's proposal for a trans-Persian railway. A group of French financiers were got to promote the scheme under some guarantee from the Russian Government, without which they would doubtless never have entertained the idea. The line was to cross hundreds of miles of desert and to cost at least £15 millions, but more probably double this amount. On another occasion (in 1911), when the British were pushing their schemes for the development of Mesopotamia and South Persia, the Tsarist Government suddenly approached the German Government, and at the famous Potsdam meeting between Kaiser and Tsar the latter offered German banking capital a share in the railway construction of North Persia. The effect was to frighten Britain for a time away from promoting any railway schemes in Persia at all.

It is no accident that railway promotions in the East form a very large part of the pre-war diplomatic conversations of the European Powers. They were either the objectives which the investment houses of the highly industrial countries of Western Europe were aiming to secure or they were the stumbling-blocks which Tsarist diplomacy was putting in the way of the Western enterprises. For Russia was the uncertain quantity in all these pre-war diplomatic games. The most easterly of Western nations and the most westerly of Eastern nations, she could not be dealt with as the effete regime of Turkey under the Sultan or of Persia under the Kajars, for she had a well-disciplined army of peasants and the beginning of a modern industry. But she could not be regarded as one of the Western Powers, for her economy was still too primitive, her higher processes of production were run by foreigners, and she was herself an unde-veloped colonial area for the investment under most profitable conditions for Western capital. She was a prize to be won by those concerned with the export of capital. But she could not be won by force, and had to be treated as an equal. The danger of conflict between a country of old capital accumulation in the A category, like Britain, and a country in the D category, like Russia, was no small one. In our classification of the countries of the world according to economic develop-ment and capital export we placed Russia fourth, behind those countries, like the British Dominions, where the conditions of the Mother Country were already developed only in embryonic state, but before those which were purely agrarian with handicraft industry, like China, Africa, and Brazil. The power of resistance of Russia to the West was greater than that of any other colonial country of Asia, and it was a resistance which aimed, as long as the agrarian nobility and the mercantile capitalists were in power in Moscow, at preventing the victorious march of industrial economy and of high finance from spreading through Asia. Modern capitalism, in fact, was too revolutionary for Tsarist Russia. Hence the points of friction between Russia and all the Powers of Western Europe in categories A and B. It may seem paradoxical, but I believe this peculiar relation between Russia and the rest of Europe was one of the most potent causes of the World War. Sir George Buchanan was telling a great truth when he said in the crisis on the eve of the outbreak of war that unless England entered the war on the side of France and Russia she would have to count on serious friction in place of co-operation with Russia in Asia. This was probably an all-important factor in deciding Britain's attitude in this crisis. The Russian nobility sought war to escape from internal revolution among the peasants; the Austrian military machine sought it to escape nationalist revolutions in the Dual Monarchy; the heavy industries of France, Germany, and England sought it to solve the problem of expansion in the East. The commercial, bondholding, and rentier classes in the three Western countries did not want it, nor did important concessionaire groups. But their voices were silenced and their agreements, with the ink scarcely dry, were torn up when the soldiers were sent marching. Among the many factors which went to make the Great War inevitable was the British fear of Russian hostility to Britain's economic interests in Asia. To buy off that hostility was the aim of British diplomacy, and a military alliance against Germany, formed under the Pact of London, was the means of binding Russia to England and of preventing her from following a policy of sabotage and obstruction in the East.

That Russian mercantile capital and the militaristic pretensions of a semi-feudal caste, together with the theocratic claims of an out-of-date Cæsarism to acquire Constantinople and become the head of a united

Eastern Church of Christendom and of a revived Holy Roman Empire, was one of the main causes of the breakdown of the economic and political *rapprochement* that was going on between the Powers of the West in 1914, there can now be little doubt. The publications of Professor Pokrovsky, to whom the Soviet Government of Russia has given the task of examining the diplomatic archives of the Tsarist Government, throw a flood of light on this aspect of pre-war Europe.[1] We saw how France had taken the lead on negotiating with Germany on disputed colonial rights, even before Britain decided to do so. Now Britain had moved towards the healing of the economic difference of pre-war capitalist Europe. That German business interests were not envisaging war we have seen in the last chapter while reviewing German capital invested in England, France, and Belgium.

Capitalistic economy was beginning to reach a stage where international agreements over colonies might have gradually superseded the stage of economic competition and nationalistic wars. Another decade of this development and war might have been outlawed as a means of settling economic problems between highly industrialized States with large capital accumulations. But the disturbing factors were the semi-feudal, theo-cratic Empires in Eastern Europe, Austria-Hungary, and Russia. It was their quarrel over Balkan claims and spheres of influence that scotched for a decade the tender plant of supernational economy that was beginning to grow in the industrial States of Western Europe.

[1] *Drei Konferenzen*, Russische Korrespondenz. Berlin, 1920; *Aus den Geheim-Archiven des Zaren*, M. Pokrovsky. Berlin, Scherl, 1920.

CHAPTER VIII

THE ECONOMIC SETTLEMENT AT THE CLOSE OF THE WAR

JUST as in the last chapter we examined the economic world tendencies which played their part in making the war in 1914, so it is expedient to pursue a similar inquiry into the peace of 1919. Under a system of competing national economies throughout the world, one need not be a cynic to subscribe to the converse of the Prussian general's dictum that peace is war carried on by other methods. During the war, diplomatic methods were at a discount. As Mr. Mowat writes,[1] "The tragic fate of diplomacy in time of war is that it has to work silently, meticulously, carefully, taking long views and therefore slowly, while every day men's lives are being lost and the degree of human anguish is deepened." Indeed, as long as the civil populations stood the strain, the General Staffs of all belligerent countries dominated policy. The short view was at a premium, the long-sighted view at a discount. So also among the heads of industry, commerce, and finance, those sections who were out for the large profits of to-day dominated over those who were more concerned to prevent an economic break-up. Moreover, once the war had started, those railway and other concession interests in England, France, and Germany, which in June 1914 were ready to come to a pacific agreement on spheres of influence in the Near and Middle East, now found it better to attain their ends by "the knock-out blow"

[1] *A History of European Diplomacy, 1914–1925.* Arnold, London, 1927.

and by "war to the bitter end." Such was the demoralization wrought by conflict over the Balkans between the military bureaucracies of Russia and Austria, that the higher economic interests of the Western and Central Powers of Europe were drawn in in sympathy, and saw their main chance now in prosecuting the war to obtain by force those spheres of interest and advantage which they would otherwise have obtained by agreement. Even the international bond-holding interests, with their branches in London, Paris, Berlin, Vienna, and New York, had temporarily to divide themselves into national watertight compartments, abandon schemes for financing Chinese enterprises or Turkish railways by international Consortiums and concentrate on floating War Bonds and "Liberty Loans" for the belligerent Governments. The artificial purchasing power thus created by the bankers was used to create unstable prosperity in the manufacture of war products, which were then blown into the air with loss to life and property. And the bondholding class in Europe, irrespective of nationality, had to look on and see prices rise and currencies inflate and the value of their bonds in terms of commodities steadily depreciate. The era of the war speculator was at hand. It was halcyon days for the armament firms, the heavy industries, the manufacturer of necessities of life and of instruments of death and the owner of raw materials. Plants were everywhere increased, new factories sprang up, industrial capital was watered to irrigate the fields of artificial prosperity.

The problem of finding markets after the war for these over-expanded war industries thus became doubly acute. The elaborate balance in capitalist economy between means of production and means of consumption, which Karl Marx elaborated so well in chapters xx and xxi of vol. ii of *Capital,* was being upset. An economic crisis more severe than any which had ever yet shaken the industrial system of Europe, and, in part, of the world, was germinating in the womb of the Great War. It was necessary to find outlets for the rapidly accumulating surplus wealth of these inflated war industries. Therefore every belligerent Government had to push for a peace settlement which would give the new industrial interests that had risen to prominence at least the same expansive outlets as they had had during the war. For with the demobilization of the armies a large part of their markets would go too, and the only alternative was to be found in large expansion of markets overseas for industrial goods and for capital investments. As far as the Allied Powers were concerned, it was possible to note three economic objectives arising out of the Peace Settlement and forming part of the economic bases of the Versailles Treaty:—

(1) The obtaining of colonial markets for commodities and for capital investment by the annexation of German colonies, by tariffs, and by the use of the League of Nations for the granting of mandates and exclusive control over transport and other concessions in the ceded territories of the Ottoman Empire and in Africa. The export of industrial surplus capital from Britain and France to colonial areas had been suspended during the war and diverted to war industry and home consumption. It had now to be resumed, and the Peace Treaty was a means to this end.

(2) As a step towards the realization of (1), the obtaining of control over the raw material resources of the Central Powers, more particularly in Lorraine, the Saar, and Upper Silesia.

(3) The obtaining of cash payments from Germany to pay interest on the war debts of the victorious countries.

It may be noted in passing that the Central Powers, if they had won the war, would certainly have developed an appetite for economic Imperialism no less than the Allies. The annexation of the coal and iron areas of Northern France, as foreshadowed in the famous Memorandum of the German industrialists to the Reichstag in 1915, and the creation of buffer States on the Western confines of Russia with German economic domination in them, as realized for a brief space in the Brest-Litovsk Treaty, would have formed the German counterpart to the economic bases of the Versailles Treaty if Germany had been victorious.

Now the three economic objectives of the Versailles Treaty proved in practice very difficult to realize. Let us consider the first objective of the dictated peace—colonial outlets for trade and capital. When the war broke out, that portion of the profits of production in belligerent countries which hitherto went either in the form of goods or of capital credits to colonial countries and dominions was now poured into war industry at home. The dearth of capital for export forced the small business communities in these colonies and dominions to start providing their own wants. So they began to accumulate surplus wealth, manufacture and create their own capital market for industry themselves. The following figures are given from a Canadian source [1] for the capital applications for Canadian enterprises before and since the war:—

Years.	From Canadian Sources.	From British Sources.
	Dollars.	Dollars.
1908–14	285,644,000	1,419,849,000
1915–18	1,487,991,000	65,775,000
1919–21	1,020,543,000	17,256,000

[1] J. Connor, of the Toronto *Forward*.

Here we see during the war years a large drop in the amount of British capital sent out to finance Canadian enterprise and an equally rapid rise in the amount supplied by Canadian capitalists themselves. The same process was going on in other fields of investment where West European capital was in the habit of moving for investment. And it was not likely that, once the native industrialists had drawn capital supplies from their own money markets, they would have the same outlet to offer to their former creditors. The inflation process of the war had made money cheap. There was plenty to lend, because currencies were depreciating and bank balances swollen artificially, but the usual outlets were being filled and new ones had not been found.[1] The Allies, particularly Great Britain, were losing these outlets for trade and investment, and against it had acquired, under the Versailles Treaty, new outlets in the mandated territories of the former German colonies in Africa and of the Ottoman Empire. But these areas were not in a position to absorb immediately large amounts of capital or of goods which formerly went to the British Dominions. Only after several years could they possibly fulfil the function of absorbers of capital and goods on a scale adequate to relieve the crisis in the Allied countries in general and in Great Britain in particular. But the problem was becoming acute and would brook no delay.

Now if we come to (2), namely, the economic objective of the Versailles Treaty which aimed at the control by Allied industrialists of the raw material of ex-enemy countries, we find that the Treaty did not solve the problem there either. Under the Spaa Agreement, which supplemented the Versailles Treaty

[1] Cf. "Economic Conference," Supplement to *Economist*, July, 1927, p. 13.

as far as concerned reparation deliveries in kind,
Germany was to deliver a certain quota in coal to
France, in order to give the members of the French
coal and metallurgical industry greater control over
the prices of metallurgical products of industry in
the Rhine basin. But no adequate arrangement
was made for coke, and the French Lorraine smelting
furnaces remained without the necessary fuel to carry
on, for the Saar coal proved to be non-coking, and
the only adequate supply came from the Ruhr ; and
the German industrialists remained in possession
of the Ruhr coke, which thus became a most important
raw material of the metallurgical industry of Central
Europe. The Versailles Treaty did not solve this
aspect of the raw material problem in the interests
of the French *Comité des Forges*. A fierce struggle
ensued between the latter in Paris and the *Reichsver-
band der Deutschen Industrie* in Berlin. The German
industrialist, Herr Stinnes, played a prominent part
between 1921 and 1923 in provoking the French to
reprisals against the German industry on the right
bank of the Rhine in the hope that they would
forcibly seize the Ruhr but be compelled to ask
assistance of the German leaders in reorganizing the
metallurgical industry of these regions, through inability
to work it themselves. Both French and German
industrialists were aiming at the creation of a kind
of Coal and Steel Consortium for both banks of
the Rhine, irrespective of national boundaries, but the
point of conflict was which of them were to be the
predominant partners. The French did actually reply
to this provocation by occupying the Ruhr in January
1923, whereby they and the Germans continued the
World War by other methods. The French captains
of heavy industry sought by military occupation of an
industrial district on the one hand, and their German

counterparts sought by passive resistance on the other, to solve their post-war problems of monopolizing the raw material resources of the Rhineland in their own interests. Though the German passive resistance was broken, the members of the *Comité des Forges* found out that they could not satisfactorily solve the problem without German co-operation. So the ground was prepared for a heavy-industry Consortium for the Rhineland, which is now slowly shaping itself. When it is formed (and we shall refer later to the developments in this direction) the second economic objective of the Versailles Treaty will have been attained, but not quite in the way the Allies intended it. For the Versailles Treaty aimed by annexation of Alsace-Lorraine, by the special regime in the Saar, by the coal deliveries, dictated at Spaa, to get complete control over the raw material resources of Western Germany for French industry. This might ultimately have occurred but for the intervention of another factor, to which we shall refer later, namely, international and particularly Anglo-American, finance.

But if economic objective No. 2 is gradually in process of attainment by modification and compromise, No. 1, the securing of markets for capital and goods of inflated war industry in colonial areas, has made but little progress. There are two principal reasons for this:

(*a*) In order to secure these outlets it is necessary for the Governments of the countries with the inflated war industries to extend their political influence over fresh colonial areas which have not yet been industrialized. We have seen above that many countries which formerly took goods and capital from Europe are now largely self-sufficing. What progress or lack of progress has been made in this direction we will examine later, in Chapter X. Suffice it here to refer to the problem and pass on to (*b*), the problem of war debts, the solution of which is hindered by the industrialists' search for new markets. And here we approach the third economic objective of those who made the Peace Treaty. There can be no doubt that the problem of war debts and the closely connected reparation payments in cash has been the cause of grave economic disturbance, although measures have been taken to mitigate its effects. Now it has become generally recognized that the payment of large reparation sums in cash from the vanquished to the victor countries was bound to cause serious depression in the industries of the countries receiving that payment. And this would only render more acute the problem of re-establishing the inflated war-time industries and providing them with outlets for goods and capital investments. For in the long run reparation can only be made by the transfer without payment of goods from one country to another. Now if the captains of war-time industry had had sole control of the policy of the Allied Governments at Versailles, doubtless we should have heard very little about payment of reparation in cash. We should only have heard about annexations of territory and about the surrendering of potential markets abroad and of raw material resources in Europe, which in fact occurred. We should have had some reparation demands, but these would have been confined to deliveries of much-needed coal, as provided for by the Spaa Agreement, and for coke, as was provided for by settlements after the Ruhr occupation. Reparations in kind would have been strictly limited, while reparations in cash, which stimulate exports of all types of goods from the conquered country, would have been recognized as a serious menace to the already threatened industries in the victor lands.

But the captains of war industry, the company promoters and concessionaires, were not alone in

influencing the policy of the Allies. The international
banking houses and the bondholding and investing
public all over Allied Europe and America, who had
on the whole been an influence against the war, and
who, when it came, had been the chief sufferers
under inflation, were now faced with a peculiar
problem of their own, which was different from, and
to some extent conflicting with, that of the captains
of industry. They had subscribed to war loans liberally
from artificial credit placed at their disposal by the
banks, they had seen their fixed interest-bearing
securities fall, as wave after wave of inflation swept
over Europe. They had seen State Budgets rise to
colossal heights and war pensions and debt services
pile up. A prospect of crushing taxation for the rest
of their days awaited them, unless they could secure
cash payments from the defeated nations which would
help to fill the gap in the State Budgets. As an example
of this, one may point to the fact that Britain's debt
to the United States equals a 7½d. in the pound income
tax. Owing to the non-payment of the continental war
debt to Britain, an additional income tax of about 1s. 11d.
in the pound is put upon the British taxpayers. This
makes a total burden of 2s. 6½d. in the pound on the
British taxpayers for the international war debt. Here,
then, was the cause of the third economic objective
of the Versailles Treaty, promulgated by the Allied
Governments in deference to the interest of the
taxpayers, bondholders, banks, and investment houses
of the Allied countries. And their political testament
is found in the pre-Armistice Note to Germany on
November 5, 1918, in the following passage: "Com-
pensation will be made by Germany for all damage
done to the civilian population of the Allies and to
their property," and in the Smuts Memorandum,
accepted by the Big Four in Paris: "This includes

all war pensions and separation allowances, which the German Government is liable to make good." Hence were formulated the schemes of cash indemnity payments by Germany to the Allied Governments. The most fantastic figures were prepared by the Allied experts in the days following the Armistice: 8,000 million sterling was to be imposed on Germany to cover the whole cost of the war to the Allies. This was scaled down in the London Ultimatum of February 1921 to 6,800 millions. These cash reparation payments were to be mortgages laid upon German industry and on the revenues of the Reich by the Allied Governments acting in the interests of their taxpayers, bondholders, and bankers.

I. THE UNITED STATES AND THE UNITED KINGDOM IN ACCOUNT WITH EACH OTHER AND WITH THEIR ALLIES IN EUROPE.

(In millions sterling.)

Creditors.	Debtors.			
	United Kingdom.	European Continent.	Total Originally Owing.	Total Actually Owing in 1927.
United States ..	900	1,048	1,948	1,948
United Kingdom ..	—	1,817	1,817	1,817 917 [1] ——— 900
Grand Total				£2,848

[1] Declared ready to annul under Balfour Note (September 1922), if continental debtors paid sum equal to debt to United States.

The enormous pressure on Germany for these payments may be explained by the fact that a similar pressure was being placed upon the Budgets and taxpayers in the Allied lands. Thus Great Britain

II. UNITED STATES AND UNITED KINGDOM IN ACCOUNT WITH THEIR EUROPEAN ALLIES SEPARATELY.

(*In millions sterling.*)

Creditors.	France.	Russia.	Italy.	Small Nations.	Total Originally Owing.	Amounts Written Off.	Total Owing in 1927.
United States ..	550	38	325	135	1,048	—	1,048
United Kingdom ..	650 150¹ —— 500	600	467 150² —— 317	100 63³ —— 37	1,817	370	1,447
Total ..	1,050	638	642	172	2,865	370	2,495

¹ Amount written off French Debt by capitalizing at 4 per cent. the difference between the interest payable under the 1925 Debt Agreement and the original amount owing.

² Amount written off Italian Debt by capitalizing at 4 per cent. the difference between the interest payable under the 1926 Debt Agreement and the original amount owing.

³ Amount written off the Small Nations' Debts by capitalizing at 4 per cent. the interest payable under agreements made up to 1927 and the original amount owing.

G

owed the United States a war debt of £900 millions, the continental Allies of Great Britain, including Russia, owed her £1,817 millions; France owed Great Britain £650 millions, France was owed by her continental Allies £355 millions. The total debt of all the Allied and Associated Powers to each other, not cancelling one against the other, amounted to £4,000 millions.

In order to get a clearer idea of the connection between Inter-Allied indebtedness and the demand for German reparations let us examine Tables I, II, III.

III. THE UNITED KINGDOM AND THE EUROPEAN ALLIES IN ACCOUNT WITH GERMANY FOR REPARATIONS UNDER DAWES PLAN.

(In millions sterling.)

Creditors.	Debtor.
	Germany.
United Kingdom	700
France	1,350
Italy	250
Small Nations	200
Total	2,500

We see here that in the course of time a considerable scaling down of values has already taken place. Great Britain in 1922 already had agreed conditionally to forgo £917 millions to her continental Allies, and only to demand the £900 millions needed to liquidate her debt to the United States. The debts of France, Italy, and of the smaller European Allies have been written down by various agreements made in recent years, which brings the total debt actually owed to Great Britain to £1,447 millions, of which £600 millions is the Russian debt, and of very doubtful value. The total actual indebtedness of the continental Allies to Great Britain and the United States, as sanctioned by agreements, comes to £2,495 millions. The payments capitalized at 4 per cent. for a full year under the latest Dawes reparation scheme for Germany come to £2,500 millions. Thus Inter-Allied indebtedness and German reparations mutually cancel, which proves that the pressure of the Allied bondholders for cash reparations payments from Germany is in direct ratio to their indebtedness to one another.

To recapitulate, therefore : the Versailles Treaty had three economic objectives :—

(1) The securing of outlets for industrial goods and capital in the interests of the war-inflated industries.

(2) The annexation of territories and economic sanctions to obtain raw-material monopoly in Europe in the interests of the same war-inflated industries.

(3) The securing of cash payments in the form of indemnities to balance Budgets in the interests of the bondholding class.

Looking back now on the events of the years from 1919 to 1923, it is possible to see that the statesmen of the Allied Powers during these years were working more for the attainment of (1) and (2) than they were for (3). They may not have known it, but the result of their efforts in slicing off parts of Germany in Silesia and Lorraine and imposing economic sanctions in the Ruhr, the result of their ruinous policy of financing Russian White armies and Greek expeditions to Asia Minor to secure outlets for goods and capital in those undeveloped areas, was to create complete industrial chaos. The owners of factories and machines are naturally more interested in rising prices for commodities than in rising values of currency, so that it was not to be expected that they would worry much about a depreciating mark and franc, or about wars and military "sanctions," which assisted this depreciation. Falling currency meant rising prices and profits. But by 1923 the Welsh advocate of "the knock-out blow," with his supporters among the upstart profiteers of war-time, the "Tiger," and Raymond Poincaré, and their backers on the *Comité des Forges*, had led Europe to a yawning abyss, from which the Russian Bolsheviks were standing ready to pull her back and clothe her in the garb of Communism. Economic objectives (1) and (2) of the Versailles Treaty had not been attained. It was time for (3) to be tried. The Lloyd George Coalition fell in 1922. The old finance, banking, landowning, royalty-levying aristocracy came into power in England, with men such as Bonar Law and Stanley Baldwin as their figure-heads. Somewhat later in France *Poincaré la Ruhr* gave place in 1924 to M. Herriot of the London Conference and the Dawes Plan. The holders in Britain of War Bonds and 3½ per cent. Conversion Loan, the French rentier-peasant, and the American of the Middle West who had subscribed to Liberty Loan, were beginning to assert their influence in the councils of Europe.

The bankers who influenced the findings of the Dawes Commission approached the economic problem, not from the point of view of securing outlets for the sale of industrial goods or of control over raw-material resources, but rather from the point of view of (3) the interests of the holders of War Bonds. They aimed at settlement of the international debt problem first and foremost. The immediate objectives which the Dawes Commission hoped to attain could be roughly divided into three parts :—

(1) The reducing of the amount of payment of reparations in kind by Germany to the Allies and the

payment of them, as far as possible, in goods which would not affect the industries of the creditor nations. This policy was clearly foreshadowed in a speech by the British Ambassador in Germany, Lord D'Abernon, to the Hamburg Chamber of Commerce in 1923, when he said: "There are many articles which we (England and Germany) can produce jointly better than we can produce them in either country separately. Where we can co-operate, let us do so."

(2) The masking of payment of reparations by Germany by letting it appear in the form of investment of capital of the creditor nations in German public works. An instance of this was the proposal to transfer the German State Railways to a private syndicate in which some of the shares should be pledged to the credit of the reparations debt. Instead of receiving increased German import of goods, the creditor countries were to receive payment in cash in interest on German railway bonds. In the long run, of course, this would mean that Germany would still have to export goods in order to get the foreign cash balances with which to pay the railway bond interest, but the idea was that the payment would be so masked as to largely mitigate its evil effects on the world markets.

(3) The attempt to spread the payment of cash reparations over as long a period as possible by scaling down the initial payments and raising them to the full amount only after four years, and also the setting up of machinery for the transfer of these cash sums so as to cause the minimum of dislocation to the international money market.

These three methods for the solution of the international war-debt problem became embodied in the Dawes Plan and were accepted after the London Conference in 1924. It involved the defeat of the policy of those industrial capitalists who would attain their ends without regard to the effects of inflated currency on the economy of Europe. It meant that they would have in future to submit to stable exchanges and the rise in the value of all fixed interest-bearing securities, loans, mortgages, and bank advances, because these only had value with a stable currency. This meant also that they could not look any more to rising prices to get out of the difficulty of finding markets for war-expanded industry. The loans which the banks had made to the heavy industries of England, France, and Germany, instead of being paid off in depreciated currency, would now have to be liquidated in currency with a gold value. The Dawes Plan was an attempt to solve the after-war economic problem of Europe by stabilizing the medium of exchange. It was the bondholders and bankers' solution. And it has certainly gone a long way to solve the problem along the lines of the objectives laid down in (3). It brings the problem of payment of war debts and reparations nearer solution. But does it bring the problem of finding investment areas for productive capital and markets for the goods of industry nearer solution? By stabilizing currency and adopting the gold standard it has solved the problem of exchange, but it remains to be seen if it has done anything for the problem of production and distribution, as enumerated in (1) and (2).

Indeed, it would seem to have made these last two problems more difficult of solution than ever. Not only has it lowered wholesale prices throughout the world and made it more difficult for war-expanded industries to find markets, but it has raised in an acute form another problem which, while connected with (1) and (2), has also some new features. The fall of wholesale prices which began in 1921 on a world scale, and applied to all countries where inflation was not being more or less deliberately practised, affected not only industrial goods, but also agricultural produce. Thus the agricultural community throughout the world was brought directly into the crisis of production in the same way as the industrial community. But the crisis in agriculture had this additional feature. Not only did it after 1921 begin to suffer from falling prices, but there began to develop a greater relative fall in prices as compared with pre-war times in the case of agricultural produce than in the case of industrial goods. This disparity began to disturb the economy of all countries in the world, as soon as they, one after the other, began to stabilize their currency and return to gold.

Thus we find in various European countries the following relation of agricultural and industrial prices :—

Germany.

1913 = 100.

			Agricultural Products.	Industrial Products.	Relation between Agricultural and Industrial Prices.
1924 ..	..	..	119·6	147·5	81·4 per cent.
1925 ..	..	..	133·0	147·1	90·4 ,,
1926 ..	..	..	129·3	137·3	94·3 ,,

N.B.—The improvement in the agricultural statistical position since 1925 is largely due to the Agrarian Tariff Law.

Austria.

(1913 = 100).

	Agricultural Products.	Industrial Products.
1923 to 1926	105·5	112·8 per cent.

Denmark.

(1913 = 100.)

	Cereal Products.	Animal Products.	Building Material.	Machines and Utensils.	Other Accessories.
1921 to 1926	211	186	272	234	224

Norway.

(1909–1913 = 100.)

	Agricultural Products.	Animal Products.	Dairy Products.	Machines and Utensils.	Building Material.
1921 to 1926	167	202	174	183	201

Holland.

(1913 = 100.)

	All Agricultural Products.	Feeding Stuffs, Fertilizers, and Wages.
1921 to 1926	158	176

Soviet Russia.

(1913 = 100.)

	Agricultural Products.	Industrial Products.	Relation between Agricultural and Industrial Prices.
1923	97	195	50 per cent.
1924	155	248	62 ,,
1925	194	230	84 ,,
1926	209	257	81 ,,

United States.

(Pre-war Average = 100.)

	Farm Products.	Clothing.	Fuel and Light.	Metals and Metal Products.	Building Materials.	House-Furnishing Goods.
Average, 1921 to 1925	140	188	189	132	174	179

Great Britain.—There are no statistics which give the position accurately. The figures for the prices of industrial products given by the Ministry of Labour (Eighteenth Abstract of Labour Statistics of the U.K., 1926) give those for depressed metallurgical trades and textiles, but are not typical of the industries which supply the farmer with most of his needs. No accurate budgeting for the receipts and payments of British Agriculture is at present possible.

Italy, Belgium, and France.—Inflation has been going on till recently in all these countries, and so comparisons are apt to be misleading.[1]

Thus it is seen that this phenomenon applies not only to countries where the form of economy after the war has not been influenced by important economic changes, but also in Soviet Russia, where great economic changes have been effected by revolution. Indeed, as is seen from the above figures, Soviet Russia suffers from the "Scissors" (the name which Trotsky gave to designate the crossing curves of prices for agricultural products and industrial goods) in the same way as the farmers in the Western States of America and the British farmer. Thus there was a new factor which has been not without influence

[1] The above figures have been worked out from a series of tables given in *Agricultural Problems in their International Aspect*, published by the International Institute of Agriculture and presented to the International Economic Conference at Geneva, June 1927.

on the politics of all countries since the years of open inflation came to an end. The agricultural communities were demanding in one way or another the closing of the "Scissors." In general it may be said that in Europe the agricultural community's influence has aimed at the continuance of price inflation in one form or another. In Germany the Junkers and the Peasants' Parties have succeeded in getting certain tariffs imposed on imported agricultural produce. The German Tariff Law of 1925 was typical of the way in which many countries in Europe tried to close the "Scissors" by using tariffs to slightly inflate prices. In most cases, however, the results were negative, because the industrial capitalists, who were also interested in inflation, managed to secure some tariffs on certain classes of their goods. Thus the one neutralized the other. In Soviet Russia attempts have been made, with varying success, to close the "Scissors" by increasing the output and so lowering the prices of the goods of the State industries. The struggle between the followers of Trotsky and the followers of Stalin inside the Communist Party of Russia is closely connected with the problem of the "Scissors." Still, the fact remains that the disparity of price between rural produce and urban goods over pre-war prices is as large as ever in most countries, and it is, no doubt, largely to be explained by the lack of selling organization on the part of the agriculturists of most lands, whereas, as we shall see in Chapter IX, the industrial captains have been able to take some steps towards meeting the deflation crisis started by the world bankers in their policy of financial stabilization. The scattered units of production and the inability to close down operations when faced by adverse markets, owing to dependence on natural processes, has put agriculture at a special disadvantage, and it has hitherto been slow to imitate urban industry in organization for selling purposes.

On the other hand, in the United States the farming community has thrown its weight into the scale of the contest between industrial and finance capital, between inflationists and deflationists in economic policy. Being, unlike the farmers of Europe, interested in the foreign market as well as in the home market, they were concerned with raising the prices of foodstuffs in Europe and pushing exports. To some extent the American banking interests coincided with this interest of the Western farmers, because they were concerned in the financing of food credits to Europe under the auspices of Mr. Hoover's organization, which did so much to fight famine after the war. Thus while the American bankers were interested in food credits for Europe, the farmers were interested in food exports to Europe, and for a time the farmers and bankers were able to march together. The American farmers, owing to the fact that they had alternate markets, were not so adversely affected by deflation as the farming community in Europe, because they were able to use the bankers' desire for food credits to Europe to push exports, whereas the European farmers had only the home market and tariffs to fall back on.

The American banks were forced to take up the question of credits to Europe by 1923. Already by that year 4,500 million dollars' worth of gold, or half the gold reserve of the world, had accumulated in the United States. The payment of debts to America, even though it had begun on a small scale by Europe at this time, had helped to aggravate the crisis due to too much gold accumulating in the vaults of the Federal Reserve Bank. There was a real danger at this time of an inflation of prices, due to too much gold being in the country. How did the American banks meet the situation, which might have led, if nothing had been done, to the wave of inflation, already threatening Europe, engulfing also America? Professor David Friday tells the story.[1] "It is clear," he says, "that the situation in America at the initiation of the Dawes Plan had in it the elements necessary for an inflation of prices both in the commodity and the security markets. . . . Everything seemed heading for prosperity, price inflation, and over-speculation on the security markets. What actually happened in the three years which elapsed since September 1, 1924? First of all, interest rates rose quickly in the call market from 2 to 4 per cent. in less than seven months after the Dawes Plan was put into operation. . . . During that period (December 1924 to April 1925) we lost 150 million dollars of gold. . . . This outflow in 1925 did doubtless help bring about the rise in money rates which occurred between the autumn of 1924 and the end of 1925."

Of course, Professor Friday goes on to point out that the export of gold to Europe did not alone prevent gold inflation in the United States during this period. The policy of lending back to Europe was supplemented by a judicious policy of credit for the home industry which enabled it to expand without inflating prices. This financial policy, coupled with the fact that the United States has a large, expanding home market and was not, like the industrial States of Europe, dependent on colonial markets for export, made possible the extraordinary after-war prosperity of the United States. But the inflation crisis in the United States, just as in Europe, was solved by the intervention of the banks. In Europe, with its relatively

[1] *Manchester Guardian Commercial*, July 28, 1927: "American Monetary Policy."

small home markets, its dependence on colonial markets, which were beginning to slip away since the war, the intervention of the banks led to deflation and the intensifying of the industrial crisis. But in the United States it simply meant that the banks rationed industrial credit. Instead of letting the American industrialists have credit at the low rates of 3 and 4 per cent. which were ruling in 1923–24, the banks started lending to Europe at the much more profitable rate of 7 and 8 per cent., and so the American industrialists had to compete for credit and had to pay 5 and 6 per cent. Thus were floated the loans which were to stabilize the German mark under the Dawes Plan, and the various advances to the Bank of France which were to prevent the franc from toppling the way of the mark. This was the economic basis of America's "return to Europe." Up till then the industrial interests in the United States had succeeded in preventing America from "becoming involved in the European turmoil," because it was to their interests to get credits from the banks at 3 and 4 per cent. But with the return to Europe of a portion of the gold which had come in payment of war debts, they no longer had a monopoly of the New York money market. The American bankers began to get the upper hand, just as their colleagues did in Europe, and they were assisted in this by the agricultural interests of the Western States, who hoped with expanding American credit in Europe to find an outlet for their surplus cereal production.

CHAPTER IX

POST-WAR ATTEMPT TO SOLVE PRODUCTION
CRISIS

WE have seen in the last chapter that the financier
or the banker who deals in credit began to exercise
a decisive influence on world economics after the
immediate post-war period had elapsed. The result
was that the owners of fixed capital, invested in
factories and machines and in the agricultural industry
all over the world, began to feel the pinch of falling
prices and higher fixed interest and rent-charges. These
owners of fixed capital had to take steps to re-establish
their position. Their first attack was, of course, upon
labour, which was made to suffer general wage reduc-
tions. Since 1921 the workers of Britain have suffered
net wage decreases of over £10 millions a week.
But this had no result in solving the problem, and,
indeed, for all industries that were manufacturing for
the home market and for agriculture it only made
the situation worse, because those whose wages were
reduced were often the best customers of the industries.
But even in the export trades, where this did not apply,
the effect was negligible. This showed that the crisis
was not only due to currency difficulties and price
deflation but, at least as far as the heavy industries
were concerned, to world production having exceeded
world demand.

Faced with this position, the owners of fixed industrial
capital began to take some steps to meet it. Up to
the present the agricultural interests have not made
any very concerted attempts to solve the problem
of how to close the "Scissors." In Britain farming

has gone from bad to worse since the intervention of the banks and the end of the post-war boom. On the other hand, the movement for organized marketing and elimination of middlemen in the handling of cereals for export has made some advance in the British Dominions, more particularly in Canada, where the Canadian Wheat Pool has been not without its influence on world prices. Somewhat similar movements are afoot in the United States and Australia.

In the sphere of urban industry more far-reaching steps have been taken by industrialists, particularly in Europe, to solve the post-war production crisis on capitalistic lines, i.e. without disturbing the existing system of ownership. The problems that had to be faced were of three kinds: (1) over-expanded productive capacity of plants, (2) under-consumption on the world markets, (3) over-capitalization of concerns during the war.

Taking (1) first, various estimates have been made of the post-war productive capacity of industrial plants. They all come in a general way to the same kind of conclusion. The German industrialist, Felix Deutsch, writing in the Berlin *Lokalanzeiger* in 1926, estimated that the total capacity of the industrial plant in the world in 1926 was 40 to 50 per cent. above the capacity for 1913. Sir Alfred Mond [1] estimated the productive capacity in the great staple industries of Europe at 30 per cent. above pre-war. As regards individual countries, a writer in the *Manchester Guardian Commercial* on December 3, 1926, estimated that the productive capacity of the British Steel plant had risen from 7·6 million tons in 1913 to 13 million in 1925, or roughly 70 per cent. Coming to (2), we can measure the under-consumption on the world markets roughly by noting how far actual production falls

[1] *The Times* for August 11, 1925.

short of productive capacity. Thus for Great Britain, France, Belgium, Luxemburg, Sweden, and the United States it has been estimated that there were the following number of blast furnaces in 1924:—

Existing	..	..	.. 1,356
Working	..	..	.. 620
Not working		..	.. 736

Again, in Great Britain alone there were 482 blast furnaces in 1924 and 1925, of which 194 were working in the first year and 169 in the second. The production of steel in Great Britain in 1923 was 40 per cent. of capacity, and in the United States 79 per cent. The steel production in Great Britain, the United States, France, Belgium, Luxemburg, Sweden, and Germany was:—

In 1915	..	..	.. 78·7 million tons
In 1924	..	..	.. 64·1 ,, ,,

The world iron production was:—

In 1870	..	..	.. 12 million tons
In 1913	..	..	.. 80 ,, ,,
In 1918	..	..	.. 120 ,, ,,
In 1923	..	..	.. 80 ,, ,,

The export of iron and steel products from all European countries in 1924 was 75 per cent. of the pre-war export. The American *Iron Age* estimated in 1925 the world production of cast iron at 59 per cent. of capacity, and of steel at 65 per cent. In shipping, also, in 1923 production was 29 per cent. of capacity in Great Britain and the United States.

On the other hand, we do not get a fair picture of the position if we look only at the heavy industries, such as coal, iron, steel, and at shipping. The League of Nations Memorandum on Production and Trade

(Geneva, 1926) gave some very interesting figures which went to show that, whereas the total population of the world in 1925 had increased 5 per cent. over the population in 1913, the index of production in all the important items of food and raw material had risen 18 per cent. above pre-war. Moreover, even in Europe, excluding Russia, where the population had increased 4 per cent., production of all these necessaries had increased by 4·5 per cent. This seems to suggest that too black a picture must not be painted and that both production and consumption have slightly risen even in Europe, whereas they have very considerably risen in certain other parts of the world. This is further borne out in the same publication by figures showing the volume of world trade in 1925 in comparison to pre-war. The following are the full figures of population, production, and trade:—

(1913 = 100.)

Continental Groups.	Population, 1925.	Production of Raw Materials, 1925.	Volume of Trade, 1925.
East and Central Europe, including Russia ..	99	102·5	73
East and Central Europe, excluding Russia ..	103	102	82
Rest of Europe	105	107	99
All Europe, excluding Russia	104	104·5	94
All Europe, including Russia	101	104·5	89
North America	119	126	137
Caribbean area	107	170	128
South America	122	134·5	97
Africa	107	138·5	99
Asia, excluding Russia ..	105	120	136
Oceania	116	122·5	132
World	105	118	105

It is clear here that Central and Eastern Europe and Western Asia have suffered more than other parts in regard to production and amount of foreign trade. But even here the position does not seem to be worse, and the amount of food and raw material that goes round per head of population seems to be slightly more than before the war. This applies mainly to Russia, Germany, Austria, and Hungary. In Western Europe the position is still better. In the North and Central American continent the position both as regards the amount available per head of population and the amount exchanged with the rest of the world has increased considerably. The same applies to Asia and in a less degree to South America. The position, therefore, which industrial capital has to face in the after-war period, when taken as a whole, does not appear in the least degree catastrophic. Taken in parts, there are weak spots, and Europe, especially certain parts of it, is the weakest. But there is nothing to suggest that industrial capital may not be able to solve its problem, if it makes certain adjustments, and it is important to see if anything in this respect is being done.

The weakest spots everywhere are undoubtedly the heavy industries. The position here is well stated in a memorandum published by a firm of London stockbrokers in December 1926,[1] on the iron and steel trades, in the following passage:—

"Increased war capacity of production has been undoubtedly one of the basic difficulties of the iron and steel trades, and, being world-wide, it is all the more difficult to cure. Under the forced draught of Governmental necessities during the war, production had outstripped normal demand by a considerable margin. This has happened before, but probably to a

[1] *The Times*, December 28, 1926.

lesser extent. It has resulted in temporary periods of depression until the ever-increasing demand for iron and steel could again absorb the supply. There is little reason to believe that the tendency for the demand for iron and steel to increase has ceased, though it has been held in check by certain post-war conditions."

The last sentence here contains an optimism which may not be justified. For although the condition of world trade and production in relation to population shows nothing catastrophic, as seen in the League of Nations figures, there *are* "certain post-war conditions" which make adjustment, especially in regard to the heavy industries, no easy matter. This brings us to (3), namely, the over-capitalization of concerns during the war. It has been estimated by Dr. Kitchen that the total value of industrial and fixed-interest securities in the world had risen from 20,000 millions sterling in 1913 to 60,000 millions in 1922. He does not state what part of this is industrial securities, but certain figures were published in the *Manchester Guardian Commercial* for December 3, 1926, for the steel trade of Great Britain, which suggest that at least as far as Western Europe is concerned a considerable portion of the increased capital, revealed by Dr. Kitchen on a world scale, can be put down to the heavy industry. Thus it is stated: "An examination of twenty-five of the largest heavy-industry firms shows two and a half times as much money in the industry in 1923 as in 1913. The output in 1913–14 was seven and three-quarter million tons, and so the output for 1923 on this reckoning, calculated in post-war values, should have been at least 19 million tons." But actually we have the following position:—

Actual output increased ..	..	8 per cent. on pre-war
Potential output increased	..	70 ,, ,,
Nominal capital increased	..	150 ,, ,,

In other words, to earn the same dividends as before, the amount of profit has to be one and a half times greater on only 8 per cent. more output!

It is here that we touch upon the crucial point in the problem of the post-war industrial crisis. Industrial capital has increased in most countries at a greater rate than either productive capacity or production. Thus, although steel production in Britain is up 8 per cent., capital invested in steel is up nearly twenty times that amount and steel prices are up 30 per cent. This 30 per cent. price increase is lower than the average price for food and raw material in the world,[1] and it explains why profits in metallurgical industries are lower than before the war, but it also helps to explain why prices are above the level that they should be if they followed only the increase of population and the increase of production. For why, in a world with population up 5 per cent. and production up 18 per cent., should average wholesale prices roughly be up 50 per cent.? Over-capitalization may not be the whole cause.[2] But it is certainly one of the causes why industrial capital seeks to re-establish equilibrium by keeping prices up.

If this were the only method, the outlook would indeed be bad. In actual fact the captains of industry in Europe are taking other, as yet, slow and indecisive but very important steps to meet the crisis of over-production, under-consumption, and over-capitalization. It is important to examine how far these steps are

[1] See League of Nations Memorandum, *op. cit.*

[2] Eugene Varga, in *International Press Correspondence*, vol. vii, No. 15, p. 298, English edition, accounts for world-price rises in the following way: "The price increase is only nominal, being based on increase of market prices during the war above production prices at the moment; these higher prices, occasioned by the shortage of goods, subsequently sterilized, passing into the production costs at each new turnover of capital."

likely to succeed. It seems that two methods have been adopted. Firstly there has been a constant tendency for tariffs to be increased to safeguard the home markets. This has been especially assisted by the political Balkanization of Europe, which has given the war-time upstart industries of the Succession States of Austria-Hungary the opportunity to shelter their inefficiency behind the artificial conditions fostered by a tariff wall. Moreover, the safeguarding duties in England, the 1926 and 1927 Tariff Laws in Germany and France, all point in the direction of securing that the depression of European industry shall at least be mitigated by securing to the home producer his own home market. This has been supplemented by the second method, which is the gradual extension of International Agreements and "Cartels." It is obvious that while tariffs help to tide over depression, as far as home markets are concerned, they can do nothing to assist a depressed industry in regard to foreign markets. And the heavy industries of the three chief producing countries of Europe—England, France, and Germany—are as much concerned with the overseas markets as they are with the home market. So it is obvious that tariffs are but pills to cure earthquakes. On the other hand, International Agreements, and the formation of organizations or "Cartels" to control output and prices and agree upon spheres of interests in overseas markets is a step which might lead to a considerable diminution of the industrial crisis.

In this respect it is noticeable that certain important steps have been taken in recent years as far as Europe is concerned. Taking the heavy industry and mining first, we may note that 1926 saw the creation of a Franco - German - Belgian - Luxemburg Steel Cartel, which has particular significance, because it was just the coal, iron, and steel interests of France and

Germany, whose competition for raw-material control in the Rhine Valley played a certain part in bringing about the European War and later the Ruhr occupation.[1] There had been agreements between the iron- and steel-masters of France and Germany before the war, but the latest agreement is certainly the most comprehensive one that there has yet been, and tends to show that the dangers of national industrial conflicts in this European area are being reduced considerably. After the liquidation of the Ruhr occupation, a German Crude Steel Association was formed during 1924 for the purpose of negotiating with foreign associations of a similar nature. In France the *Office de Statistique des Produits Métallurgiques* was formed for similar purposes. The whole question of eliminating Franco-German competition on neutral markets in metallurgical products was closely connected with tariffs. The first thing to be done was to prevent the dumping of French metal wares in Germany and German in France, and a beginning in this direction was successfully carried out in a Provisional Agreement which was signed in June 1924. Under this agreement Germany granted France an import into Germany of one and three-quarter million tons of pig iron and metal wares at the minimum tariff, the German importers paying half the duty. The rest of the German home market was left to the German iron-masters, who acquired also a monopoly of handling French imports. If German output fell below a certain figure, French imports were automatically restricted. France, on the other hand, gave Germany the minimum tariff to German exports—on condition, however, that they were sold abroad at prices ruling normally in the Dutch ports. But the German iron-masters wanted to go farther. They wanted a general reduction of output in Europe

[1] See Chapter VIII.

to prevent production from continuing to outstrip consumption. This aim was not achieved till later.

It was not till the autumn of 1926 that the first real step was taken towards the so-called "rationalization" of production; that is, the bringing of production and consumption into closer relations with one another in regard to metal wares on the Continent. It was then that the Franco-German-Belgian-Luxemburg Steel Cartel was formed. After protracted negotiations, the iron-masters of these countries agreed to limit mutually the amount of steel produced in their respective countries. It was agreed that the total output of steel should be not more than $27\frac{1}{2}$ million tons, to be distributed in the following quota for each country:—

Germany	..	..	42·7 per cent.
France ..	..	..	30·8 ,,
Belgium	..	..	12·5 ,,
Luxemburg	..	..	8·15 ,,
Saar ..	..	..	5·7 ,,

Fines were imposed upon those countries exceeding this quota. For every ton produced one dollar was paid into a common pool and the producer received this back at the end of the year, but if he exceeded his quota he paid a fine of 4 dollars a ton for every ton excess, and this was deducted from the amount due to him at the end of the year.

It is thus seen that a total output of $27\frac{1}{2}$ million tons will be confined to these countries in Western and Central Europe. This is no reduction on their normal production, but it is at least a prevention of further cut-throat competition, tariff wars, price or wage cuts, in the steel trade. If the price is estimated at £5 a ton, that will mean a turnover of £150 millions a year. Should it be decided in future to reduce the total output from $27\frac{1}{2}$ to 20 million tons, this might easily bring with it a rise of at least 20 per cent. in the price of steel and add some £20 millions on to the value of the steel turnover in these countries. Thus, we see that the Continental Steel Cartel, while it has created machinery for bringing production and consumption into closer relations, has done nothing to bring consumption into relation with prices, for its probable ultimate effects will be to increase steel prices, unless some outside influence, such as public control through the League of Nations, is brought to bear on it.

Before passing on to the other international industrial agreements it may be mentioned that a similar "Cartel" has been formed between the iron-masters of Czecho-Slovakia, Austria, Hungary, and Rumania. The agreement is to prevent price-cutting on the East European markets. Negotiations have been also in progress towards bringing the iron-masters of these countries into the larger West European Steel "Cartel." The latter controls about 30 per cent. of the world's steel production, while the United States controls some 50 per cent., and the balance is produced in Great Britain and the East. There is as yet nothing approaching a world organization for the control of production and prices in crude iron and steel. On the other hand, unofficial negotiations have been going on for the inclusion of Great Britain in the Continental Steel "Cartel," and time may ultimately bring about a movement towards agreement between the European and the American producers.

As regards other branches of heavy industry there is as yet no organization for the control of coal production as there is for steel and iron products. In Germany a national organization, the *Reichskohlensyndikat*, is in existence which controls the amount of coal produced nationally, and in France a looser organization performs to some extent this function. Also, the various reparations agreements under the Peace Treaties control the amount of coal and coke passing between Germany and the continental Allies. The great stumbling-block to a successful organization for controlling the production of coal and rationing markets is the British coal-owners, whose whole businesses are built up on the antiquated individualist methods of early Victorian capitalism, which continental capitalists have abandoned long ago. The whole principle of beggar-my-neighbour and of price-cutting by small inefficient concerns is rampant among coal producers in Great Britain and has become something of a European scandal. Of all the branches of heavy industry, coal is the most in need of a more rational organization, and this is the one thing which may still save much of the capital invested in coal. On the continent of Europe this is being slowly done, and we shall probably see in the course of a few years a widespread organization for the rationalization of the production and consumption of coal. In Great Britain alone the coal industry is plunging into a catastrophe which only State interference and public control can avert.

As regards other mineral products and raw material of heavy industry it is necessary to mention three international agreements. The first is the Franco-German Potash Cartel. This was reconstructed soon after the war, and was amended last in April 1927; thereby the potash industries of France and Germany agreed not to invade each other's markets and also agreed to share the world markets on the basis of 50 per cent. for each contracting party. Since France and Germany control over 90 per cent. of the potash production of the world, this agreement may be regarded as setting up a world monopoly in potash.

Secondly, there is the International Copper Syndicate, which was formed in 1927 among copper producers in Great Britain, the United States, France, Germany, and Africa. Not many details are known about the agreement, but it is understood to aim at stabilizing copper prices, at eliminating speculation, and at doing away with middlemen. The syndicate controls 90 per cent. of the copper production of the world, and so can be said to constitute a virtual world monopoly.

Thirdly, there is an international agreement in respect of another important raw material, namely, aluminium. At the end of 1926 the producers of Great Britain, France, Germany, and Switzerland signed an agreement for the regulation of prices, interchange of technical information, and for the division of markets. Austrian and Italian aluminium producers are also involved in virtue of capital participation in France and Switzerland. This agreement, however, only covers about 45 per cent. of the world production of aluminium, since the rest is in American hands and is outside the agreement.

The tendency towards over-production of oil and competition with artificial oils from the distillation of coal has brought together the oil producers of the world, outside Soviet Russia, to negotiate on questions of prices and, at least in regard to some of the refined products of crude oil, tentative agreements have been reached. Recently a Benzole Agreement has been signed covering Europe, with a view to regulation of competition in these markets by the big oil concerns. Also the Dutch Royal Shell and the American Standard Oil have got agreements with the German Chemical Trust for a 25 per cent. participation in the exploitation of artificial benzole on the world markets.

Coming now to international agreements on manufactured goods, there is an important agreement to regulate the production and price of steel rails. The parties to it are the rail manufacturers in Great Britain, France, Germany, and Luxemburg. The United States regard the agreement with "benevolent neutrality." The home markets are reserved for the manufacturers of each of these countries, and foreign markets are divided on an agreed basis.

An agreement with regard to the manufacture and price for tubes has come into force between manufacturers in Czecho-Slovakia and Germany to which France, Austria, and Poland are parties. A similar agreement exists for rolled-wire manufacturers in Belgium and Germany. Enamel ware manufacturers in Germany, Austria, Hungary, Czecho-Slovakia, and Poland are associated in a combine which rations contracts and arranges prices and sales on joint export markets. The manufacturers of incandescent lamps in Great Britain, France, Germany, Holland, Scandinavia, Italy, Japan, and the United States are associated in a loose type of convention which guarantees the home markets for each of the contracting parties.

Coming to another type of agreement, namely, that concerned with the marketing of products of the soil, we can take note of the well-known International Rubber Restriction Agreement, or the Stevenson Scheme. According to this the rubber products of the British Empire are controlled as regards the amount which may be placed on the market, the quota varying with the world price of the article. As Holland is not party to this agreement, its effect has not been wholly that which the promoters desired. Certainly it has tended to keep the price of rubber up, but there has developed since the boom year of 1925 a constant sagging tendency, due to the lack of watertightness in the scheme, and the Dutch planters have hastened to make use of their freedom to export to the world market as much as they desire.

A somewhat similar restriction scheme in regard to raw sugar is in operation in Cuba, but the effect in stabilizing world prices for sugar is still wanting. Other sugar-producing countries have not joined in. Attempts, so far unsuccessful, have been made to control the price of raw cotton in Egypt and America, and also the price of raw silk by producers of Japan. As regards cotton, British industrial interests are concerned in preventing a cotton price restriction scheme, as the American rubber users are to prevent the rubber restriction scheme from being a success. In each case the producers favour production restriction and the users oppose it.

Perhaps the most important of all in this category is the Canadian Wheat Pool. It is the first real attempt on an international scale to deal with the problem of the "Scissors," to which we referred in the last chapter. The Canadian farmers have now got control of 60 per cent. of the Canadian harvest and are marketing it direct to Europe. They are endeavouring to bring in the United States, Australian, and Argentine wheat producers. So far the Pool only aims at getting rid of the middlemen who take such heavy toll of the price of their products, but in time the necessity will be felt to bring the production of wheat into relation with world consumption, and to prevent over-production and price falls. But since agriculture is a process covering a whole year, and is much exposed to weather conditions, it is much more difficult to bring production into relation with consumption than is the case with manufacturing industries.

We have seen enough from the above agreements to make it clear that a certain amount has been done by capital invested in industry and agriculture throughout the world to rationalize production and bring some order into the problem of marketing. But much more remains to be done. The aims of these agreements may be summarized as follows :—

(1) To keep world prices and output steady.

(2) To protect home markets for home producers by arranging spheres of interest.

(3) To prepare the way for the writing down of watered capital by the creation of syndicates which may ultimately lead to international capital amalgamations.

Before closing this chapter it must be recalled that the Geneva Economic Conference dealt with the problem of International Industrial Trusts. The resolution which was finally passed gave only conditional approval of their formation and activities. But such approval as was given indicated that the Conference was not solely concerned with getting rid of tariff barriers, but was prepared to consider the "rationalization" of industry on the basis of international agreements. There can be no doubt that the days of doctrinaire Free Trade are coming to an end. If order is to be created in industry, if production is to overcome the post-war crisis, there must be interference with the crude operations of the law of supply and demand. Free Trade and cut-throat competition is to-day as dangerous, ineffective, and anarchical as are tariffs. International agreement and regulation of the amounts of import and export between nations, according to a definite plan, based on consumers' needs, the establishment of the quota system in international trade—all these constitute interference in the freedom of trade, but are some of the means by which industry can overcome the post-war production crisis.

CHAPTER X

POST-WAR ATTEMPT TO SOLVE THE DEBT PROBLEM

IN the last chapter we showed that industrial capital has been making certain attempts to deal with the crisis of production since the war. It will have been noted that one of its methods aims at bringing production down to the level of the existing world consumption. No attempt is made to bring the consumption up to the level of productive capacity, nor even, for that matter, to existing production. On the other hand, we have seen in Chapter VIII that the solution of the international war debt question and of German reparations, with which it is intimately bound up, will require, even after the modifications which are inherent in the Dawes Plan, the increase of production for export of the heavy and manufacturing industries of Germany, the chief debtor State. But if the aim of European industrial capital is to overcome its production crisis by promoting international agreements and "Cartels" for regulating production on an international scale, the attainment of this object will be rendered more difficult if one of the chief industrial countries of Europe, which also happens to be the chief debtor nation, is compelled to increase its production far in excess of the amount which the international agreements aim at. For instance, if the European Steel "Cartel" continues to function satisfactorily, and even to extend its membership, its tendency will be rather towards reducing the amount of metal wares which Germany exports to the foreign markets and the German members of the "Cartel" will be confined more to the home market. This will knock the bottom out of attempts to get Germany to pay reparations by the export of metal wares. But how else can Germany pay except in manufactured goods of some sort? For she is not, like Russia, a raw-material exporting country. Here is what Marxists can correctly point to as the "dialectical contradiction" in the economic system, which, if it cannot be solved, must lead to a crisis and ultimate collapse through inherent inconsistencies. On the other hand, there are signs which seem to point to a solution of the crisis which, while ultimately modifying the economy of Europe and to a lesser extent of the rest of the world, will do so without any spectacular breakdown. Thus Marx may be vindicated after all, though some of his present-day followers in Moscow may not be.

We have already seen in Chapter VIII that the international banking authorities in the United States and Great Britain have got a scheme into operation for modifying the original plan of reparation settlement promulgated at Versailles. Side by side with this has taken place the American "return to Europe," while the Federal Reserve Board has used America's gold reserves to prevent financial chaos and promote stabilization in Europe. But we seem to be on the eve of a more far-reaching change than this. The continent of Europe, and to a smaller extent Great Britain, has been cleared of much of the mushroom industrial growths of the war period. The inflated concerns which lived on speculation and currency depreciation, such as the Stinnes Concern in Germany and those of Bosel and Castiglioni in Austria, have disappeared. The decisive voice in German politics to-day is that of the President of the Reichsbank, Herr Schacht. In Great Britain it is the Bank of England and the "Big Five" rather than the Federation of

British Industries that influence the policy of the Treasury. But, further than this, finance is cautiously launching out into new industrial enterprises. In Germany the heavy metallurgical industries are losing much of their former dominating influence on politics. Large new industrial forces have accumulated since 1926 round the great German Chemical Trust, so-called *Interessengemeinschaft Farbenindustrie*, which has been largely brought into existence by the capital accumulations subscribed by the German banks. In Great Britain the principle of financial trust companies is steadily spreading. The investing public is less inclined to leave its savings in War Loan and gilt-edged stock, and is inclined to speculate mildly in industry, whereby it tries to spread its risks. There has been since the war a very considerable increase in this type of company, which is half industrial and half financial. The people that control these companies and use the savings of the investing public are concerned in pushing new industries, which in many cases are quite outside the sphere of the old staple industries, like cotton, coal, engineering, and steel. It is only necessary to mention artificial silk, electricity, electro-chemistry, to indicate the channels into which much new capital is flowing. Some finance capital is ceasing to be solely of the pure bondholder type, and is penetrating the new industrial processes which scientific invention has brought within the bounds of commercial possibility. It has, therefore, an interest in industrial prosperity. It is not solely concerned with being the receiver of fixed interest, of promoting the rise in the value of currency and the fall in prices. It favours stabilization to-day, whereas four years ago, when the inflation wave was submerging Europe in chaos, it prescribed the medicine of deflation and by so doing brought on a grave industrial crisis. Moreover, the capitalist class in Britain to-day are inclined more to spread their risks, and to hold a portion of the capital in fixed-interest stock, which is secure under deflation, and a portion in industrial securities through investment trusts, whereby it is secure if a wave of inflation should come again. Up to now we have spoken of industrial capitalists and finance capitalists as if they were two different persons. This was largely true up till quite recent times, and, moreover, for the purposes of this inquiry it served to show the conflict of economic interests that arose between war profiteer and bondholder at the Peace Conference. But to-day it is not strictly correct to speak as if they are two persons. To a certain extent they may be still. For instance, the joint-stock banks and insurance companies must still be mainly bondholders. But a large number of investment houses in the City are now concerned in financing industrial enterprises at home or abroad. Hence the boundary between bondholding and industrial capital cannot be clearly drawn.

In the United States, also, somewhat of a revolution has been going on in the mode of capital investment. Formerly the American public would not look at foreign loans. The home money markets swallowed all the public could offer. But the stream of gold which has poured into America, and the need for America to find capital outlets, has created an investing public which subscribes to capital issues abroad.

Thus the tendency in Britain for finance capital to penetrate the new industries and the tendency of the American public to subscribe to foreign loans has led to (1) a desire to assist an industrial revival in Europe by credit facilities; (2) a fear of aggravating the industrial crisis by forcing still further a policy of currency deflation; (3) the placing of a part of

America's gold reserve at the disposal of European Governments and industry to tide over the difficult period of reconstruction. This process of the return of gold from the United States to Europe began in 1924. Thus during that year 600 million dollars had gone to Europe, against nothing in the previous year.[1] In 1925, also, 920 million dollars of American capital came to Europe. Great Britain also exported some capital to Europe during these years, but relatively to the United States only a very small amount. In 1919 England's investments in Europe (excluding war loans) were £184 millions, in 1925 £274 millions—a rise of £90 millions. Since then more has gone.[2]

The object for which capital went to Europe during this period was at first to support the European currencies. Thus in 1924 20 million sterling went from the United States to Germany under the Dawes Plan, and was used as a basis for the new German currency and to enable Germany to meet her liabilities. This was a currency stabilization loan. In the same year 20 million sterling went to France to support the franc. Other smaller amounts of American capital have gone for similar objects to Italy, Belgium, Greece, Poland, Austria and Hungary. Since one country after another in Europe has abandoned inflation and set out upon the path of stabilizing its currency, the demand for gold as a backing for the new currency has increased. This brings about a new situation which is not without its dangers. The wave of nationalism which swept over Europe during the war left behind it an aftermath of Succession States from the Irridentist provinces of the former Central Powers and of Russia. Each

[1] *Economist*, June 25, 1927, "America's Foreign Investments."
[2] See Chapter XI.

of these States set about to enclose its boundaries with tariff walls. This has helped to bring about the decline of European trade. But even worse has been the effects in the region of finance, for the rise of petty nationalism and the Balkanization of Europe has brought about a desire on the part of the new countries to possess their own gold reserves as a backing for their currencies. If tariff walls and currency inflation was the fashion from 1914 to 1922, so from 1924 to the present time a hunt for gold as backing for currency is characteristic of the stabilization period. Now the gold production of the whole world has not risen since the war to a sufficient degree to meet this new demand. The increased demand may therefore lead to a fresh deflation. It would lead to continuous fall in prices of commodities due to an inordinate rise in the value of gold. Thus Europe would jump from the frying-pan into the fire, and the return of America's gold to Europe would not save her from the disastrous consequences of a long period of deflation of prices and trade depression such as went on from 1880 to 1895. The solution of the problem of production which we discussed in the last chapter would be farther off than ever.

This serious prospect may, however, be eliminated if America grants credits to Europe based on gold which remains in New York. If, for instance, a Succession State wishes to stabilize its currency, it is possible for it to borrow from New York without any gold leaving for Europe. This is called the "gold exchange standard," for the gold is earmarked in New York as backing for the loan, but it does not cause a psychological panic by a hunt for gold on the money markets of the world, which has such evil effects on commodity prices and so on the industrial situation. The chief difficulty in getting the gold exchange

standard to work in Europe will be the national pride
of the small Succession States, all of whom want their
own gold reserve and consider dependence on gold in
America beneath their dignity. But it seems that the
United States at least is moving in the direction of a
policy which grants credits to Europe on the basis
of gold in America rather than of export of gold
itself. Thus from 1924 to 1926 the United States lost
150 million dollars of gold which was exported to
Europe. But in 1926 and 1927 over 200 million flowed
back to America again, while her loans to Europe
showed no signs of decreasing.[1] Since the first rush
of stabilization fever has past, American financial
help to Europe has taken the form of credit mainly,
the gold tending to remain in America and even to
increase accumulating there. This means, then, that the
United States remains in possession of at least one
half of the gold reserve of the world, but that an increasing portion of it is now used to back loans to
Europe, instead of, as before 1924, acting only as
backing for internal loans to American industry, or
else lying useless in the safes of the bank. Now it is
obvious that if this is the case the United States
have the very greatest interest in securing that other
countries should return to the gold standard as the
basis of their currency. For thereby New York, which
has the bulk of the gold reserve in the world, can
control the financial policy of the rest of the world
and indirectly influence production and distribution.
The hunt for gold to stabilize currencies may lead
either to the establishment of national gold reserves
throughout the world, a large rise in the price of gold
and the fall of commodity prices with all its attendant
ills on world trade, or it may lead to a situation in

[1] "America's Monetary Policy," by Professor David Friday,
Manchester Guardian Commercial, July 28, 1927.

which the gold is rationed out sparingly and made the basis for a larger currency than would otherwise be the case. In a way, of course, this last is an attenuated form of inflation, but one which is not accompanied by any ill effects to the industrial systems of the world. Moreover, it is one thing to use as a basis for credit gold lying idle, as in the United States, and quite another to expand credit artificially on the basis of a limited gold reserve, as some monetary reformers would have this country do. That would be real inflation with all its attendant evils. The political effect of America's loan policy in Europe is likely to be that she will of necessity become more and more interested in the affairs of other countries, and the era of American isolation is drawing to a close through economic causes. There are now few international loans in which the United States has not got some share, and the interests of Wall Street must become increasingly a concern of United States foreign policy. If there is change of Government in Greece, Washington will be there to see its effects on the financial position of the country and the prospects of meeting the interest on loans. If thirty years ago it was London that fulfilled this rôle to such a degree that the American Press used to talk of the "financial dictation of London," and Bryan crusaded against the gold standard, whose jealous guardian was then in London, and cried out about "crucifying mankind upon a cross of gold," to-day that rôle is being assumed by the United States herself.

Not that London is altogether without its former influence upon the financial market of the world. Britain's proximity to Europe and the experience of British bankers in foreign finance make London still one of the two great financial centres of the world, but undoubtedly it is now unable to do without

American co-operation what formerly it could do by itself. The finance aristocracy of Britain, the landed and official classes, have always maintained close connection with the great republic of the New World. A portion of the liquid securities of the families of the nobility are invested across the water. Anglo-American co-operation is as marked in the region of international finance as competition is in the region of industry. This can be seen from the fact that at the time when America was returning to Europe and putting her gold reserves behind the currencies of Europe, thereby calling forth a fall in commodity prices and a first-class industrial crisis, at this time Great Britain chose to return to the gold standard and to force the pound sterling back to parity with the dollar. This policy was clearly in the interest of the holders of fixed-interest securities both here and in the United States, because it gave all bonds of this kind a backing measured in gold. But the policy of artificially forcing the sterling back to parity with the dollar, from a level of about 4 dollars 40 cents to 4 dollars 80 cents, only intensified the trade depression in England. It made foreign goods cost less at home, it is true, but it made home goods cost more abroad. Welsh coal in South America rose 10 per cent. in price in consequence of this financial operation. It hit all industries working for the world markets. It provided a premium for imports and a discount for exports.

Moreover, the existing parity exchange value of the pound with the dollar is not justified by the economic position of Britain. The active trade balance of the country has become steadily less and less, and was least of all at the time when Britain was returning to the gold standard and forcing the pound up to parity. Allowing for the invisible exports such as shipping profits, insurance, freights, interest on foreign investments, we find a trade balance for the following years:—

1922	..	..	..	£ + 154	millions
1923	..	..	..	£ + 102	,,
1924	..	..	..	£ + 86	,,
1925	..	..	..	£ + 54	,,
1926	..	..	..	£ − 12	(passive)
1927	..	..	..	£ + 96½	millions

This steady fall in the real trade balance of Britain shows that the difference between what she produces and what she consumes was diminishing just in those years when her currency was rising, from 4 dollars 40 cents to the pound to 4 dollars 80 cents. Could anything prove better that the rise in the currency of Britain is an artificial one, fostered by sentiment and "pegged" at its present high level by interested parties? If left to itself, 4 dollars 40 cents to the pound is more probably the level at which sterling should have remained, and there was nothing to prevent its having been devalued and fixed at that level of exchange when Britain returned to the gold standard. If this had been done, the country would have had the advantage of the gold standard, and the relative stability which goes with it, with none of the evils of a deflation crisis in industry. It had already suffered one such crisis in 1921, and now in 1925 and the following years it was to suffer from an aftermath of the first crisis. As Professor Schumpeter of Bonn University put it in a paper at the British Association at Leeds in September 1927: "Among the external causes of instability in the case of England is the policy of deflation through the restoration of the gold standard to parity with the dollar *before the purchasing power of the pound had reached normal level.*" (My italics.) But this policy has enhanced the value of the interest received by the holders of the National Debt by some 10 per cent., i.e. by about 50 million sterling a year! And to force this hothouse plant of dollar-sterling parity to grow, recourse was obliged to be had to the American gold reserve. For, as Mr. Churchill stated in his Budget speech in April 1925, when announcing the return to the gold standard, a gold credit of 200 million sterling would be placed at the disposal of the Bank of England by the Federal Reserve Board of America, and 100 million sterling by the house of Pierpont Morgan, if this should be needed to prevent the pound from falling from parity. Thus American gold is being used to bolster up the pound, as it is in the case of the other currencies of Europe. Only in the case of Britain it is a credit which is locked up and not actually made use of, as in the case of the others who have to pay interest on loans. But the effect is much the same, for no doubt the knowledge of this financial backing which the Bank of England has in New York provides the psychological stimulus which keeps the pound at parity, although the industrial and commercial balance of the country does not warrant it. It is also possible to argue that dollar-sterling parity might have been attained without this painful deflation method at all, by doing nothing to affect the exchange between England and America, and by allowing the gradual rise in prices in America, resulting from trade prosperity, to bring the price levels of the two countries together and so the exchanges to parity.

But let us now return to the effect of the extended credits of America to Europe. How is this going to influence the problem of war debts and reparation payments? The United States is owed by Europe a capital sum of £1,948 millions. If we calculate interest at 5 per cent. and sinking fund at 2 per cent. per annum, this will give us a figure of about 650 million dollars, or £133 millions which ought annually to be paid by Europe to America. But the United States banks have lent £600 millions more in 1924 to Europe and have received back only the annual payment from Great Britain in interest and sinking fund on the war debt. This means that Europe owed the United States, at the end of 1924, £1,948 millions plus £120 millions, i.e. £2,068 millions. And during 1925, 920 million dollars, or £180 millions, was lent to Europe, thus increasing the debt owed by Europe to £2,248 millions. Of course, it is probable that the rate of lending to Europe will slow down considerably in view of the passing of the stabilization crisis. But there is as yet no sign that the amount which America receives from Europe in interest and sinking fund is going to exceed, or even equal, as yet the amount which represents the interest on the sums she lends Europe every year. Thus a wholly anomalous situation is being created. For at the end of 1924 the United States, instead of being owed by Europe £133 millions interest and sinking fund, was owed £142 millions. At the end of 1925, instead of being owed £142 millions, she was owed £154 millions. Indeed, it has been estimated by Sir Josiah Stamp [1] that American capital invested abroad will have amounted in twenty years to 4,000 million sterling, in thirty years to 8,000 million, and in fifty years to 26,000 million, if this principle of the re-investment back to Europe of all that is owing by Europe to America is continued.

On a smaller scale altogether the same thing might be said to be going on in the case of Great Britain's war debts, owed to her by the Continent. In 1924 she was receiving nothing on account of these debts in interest, whereas in the same year she subscribed to the Dawes loan to Germany £12 millions, and thereby

[1] *The Annalist*, October 30, 1925, p. 539.

increased Europe's indebtedness to her from £1,817 millions to £1,829 millions. In 1925 and 1926 further loans to European Governments and municipalities amounted to £20 millions, thereby raising the total indebtedness of Europe to £1,849 millions. In the meantime, however, reparation payments have been begun by Germany, and this has somewhat reduced this figure. Still the principle remains true in the case of Great Britain, as with the United States, only of course on a smaller scale, that the debtor nations of Europe are being lent money by their creditors to pay their war debts. This leads to altogether absurd results, and has only this advantage to the creditors, that they are able to use political influence on the debtor Governments, and so prepare the way for their economic penetration at a later date.

This economic penetration has already been going on on a small scale, as far as Germany is concerned. Thus in 1925 the following German industries and banks took up loans in the United States:—

Krupps	£500,000
Thyssen	£600,000
A.E.G.	£500,000
Siemens	£500,000
Deutsche Bank	£2 millions
Rheinische-Westfalische Electric Works	£2 millions
Osram	£1 million
Hamburg-American Line	£1 million
Textile Bank	£1 million
Potash Loan	£6 millions
West German Mining Trust	£6 millions
Various municipalities	£6 millions

In the following year (1926) £50 millions American capital went into German industries alone in the form of short and long term credits. Since then, however, there has been a slowing down of these types of loans to German industry, and a good deal more buying of German municipal bonds and shares in German industry which have been issued on the New York Stock Exchanges has been going on. But how much this amounts to is very difficult to estimate.

The net result of these loans to German industry and to the German Government and municipalities has been to still further increase German indebtedness to her creditors. Instead of paying off her reparations debt, she has increased it, for what little she has paid off has been done largely with the aid of the cash provided by these foreign credits. Thus although the payment plan under the Dawes Scheme has been only £50 millions in 1924–25, £61 millions in 1925–26, and £75 millions in 1926–27, while the full year's payment of £125 millions is not due till 1928–29, still Germany has not been able to meet these smaller payments without borrowing. Thus in 1926 she borrowed in all £80 millions from abroad, while she paid under the Dawes Scheme £75 millions. It is obvious that this cannot go on. Germany cannot go on borrowing to pay the reparation debts, any more than the European Allies can go on borrowing indefinitely to pay their war debts to America, unless the whole economy of the world is going to become top-heavy, the burden of indebtedness increase to such a degree that industry is hampered, and taxation raised to a pitch which no people can tolerate. Well may Mr. Garvin have written in the *Observer*,[1] "No human soul born since 1900 in any country can be held responsible for the war. Even in ten years from now the vast bulk of the burthen of the debts and indemnities will be borne throughout Europe by people who were only in their early teens when the war broke out. . . . Will all these systems and debt settlements go on smoothly according to programme up to 1980 or 1990? We do not believe it."

[1] August 23, 1925.

It is still possible, of course, that Europe's debt to America may be partially liquidated, not solely by cash payments and the export of goods, but by personal services in the form of tourist traffic, etc. Some interesting figures in this connection have been given in the publication on America's Balance of Payment issued by the United States Department of Commerce. The Balance of Receipts and Payments by and to the United States for 1925 is shown in the table on p. 141.

It is here seen, firstly, that Europe seems to be paying, all told, to America slightly less than America is lending back to Europe; and, secondly, that it has been possible for Europe to pay to America during 1925 the sum of 660 million dollars on account of tourist traffic of Americans visiting Europe, and 310 million dollars on account of immigrants' remittances—a total of 970 million dollars, or about £190 millions. Furthermore, Mr. Hoover is credited with a plan for dealing with the reparation and debt problem. According to him and to other American economists, the industrial countries of Europe are better able to specialize in the manufacture of fine instruments requiring special technique, while America confines herself to large-scale production of the commoner articles of use. Europe might, according to this view, provide many specialities to the world by way of export which might go against reparations account. As regards Germany's side of the international debt problem, her annual payments should be capitalized in a lump sum and lent by America and Great Britain to Russia, Rumania, and other undeveloped Eastern countries, with the object of developing railways and other public works. German industry would then be engaged in working on the materials needed for the construction of these works and the proceeds would be credited to reparations account. The reason why

(In millions of dollars.)

Items.	Exports (Credits).	Imports (Debits).	Balance.
Visible Items.			
Merchandise	4,934	4,268	+ 666
Invisible Items.			
Interest on inter-Allied debt ..	160	—	+ 160
Private interest and dividends..	520	165	+ 355
Ocean freights	75	83	— 8
Government payments ..	—	5	— 5
Services to tourists	100	660	— 560
Charitable and missionary expenditure	—	50	— 50
Immigrants' remittances ..	—	310	— 310
Motion-picture royalties ..	75	—	+ 75
Total invisible and visible items	5,864	5,541	+ 323
Movement of Capital.			
New foreign loans, exclusive of refunding	—	920	— 920
Sale and purchase of outstanding securities	411	90	+ 321
Foreign bonds paid off.. ..	140	—	+ 140
Principal of inter-Allied debt ..	27	—	+ 27
United States paper currency ..	—	62	— 62
Total capital movement ..	578	1,072	— 494
Gold and Silver Movements.			
Gold	262	128	+ 134
Silver	99	65	+ 34
Total gold and silver	361	193	+ 168
Total of all items	6,803	6,806	— 3

Russia and the Near and Middle East are chosen for Germany is because of her proximity to these undeveloped areas, and of the fact that her industrialists are well acquainted with these markets. The obvious difficulty here would be that as long as the financial blockade of Soviet Russia continues the credits necessary for this construction work would be difficult to obtain. It is a case here of the old bondholders, interested in the Russian Government's securities of pre-revolutionary times, obstructing the international debt solution of the new bondholders, who aim at controlling the new industrial developments of the world from America and England. It remains to be seen if this obstruction is likely to be worn down in the course of time. But if this solution is possible for German reparations, there is no reason why it should not be possible for the European Allies' debt to America. It has been suggested in the same quarters in America that the United States might grant large credits to countries like Brazil, Australia, and the Argentine to increase the productivity of these countries in raw material which the United States might absorb in the form of wool, rubber, and sugar, and this might be set against European debt account. Europe might provide the public works which are needed in these countries to make this increased production of raw material possible. This again might be a feasible way out, if the objection of American industry could be overcome. For American industry is certainly looking to these countries as an outlet for its surplus wares which are not consumed at home, and sooner or later an over-production crisis is likely to come to the home market of the United States. If, therefore, the scheme to work off German reparations in Russia and the Near East is difficult to achieve, because of the obstruction of the old Tsarist bondholders, so is this latter scheme not easy, unless the financial interests in New York are able to make the industrial interests of Chicago and Detroit toe the line. It is, however, not impossible that this obstruction may be overcome and a solution of the debt and reparations problem found along these lines. One thing is certain, namely, that the best brains of the capitalist world, like Sir Josiah Stamp and Mr. Hoover and many others, are working at this problem.[1]

But when all these methods have been tried, it is still doubtful if a solution will be found which will make it possible to transfer such a vast quantity of goods as are represented in the reparation and war debt figures to markets which are in need of them. It is very doubtful if markets of this volume are to be found in the present state of world production and consumption, as outlined in Chapter IX. Nevertheless there is another card which the financial controllers of contemporary world economy have up their sleeves. They can agree to a gradual scaling down of the reparations and war debts. As Mr. Garvin hinted in 1925, the burden of debt is unlikely to be borne indefinitely by the rising generation. But already there are signs that opinion is being prepared for a cancellation of a portion at least of this international indebtedness. Thus as far back as January 2, 1925, *The Times* financial correspondent wrote: "The debts of the United States, and in general all international war debts, must be put into one general account, or, to use a popular term, they must be pooled. . . . If the United States consented to a scaling down, for example, by reduction of interest payable, the surplus obtained could be applied to increasing the sinking fund of the debt." Again, on October 2, 1925, the Paris correspondent of *The Times* wrote: "There is a conviction abroad which is shared by some very

[1] For further information about proposed methods of settling international debt and transfer problems, see *Europas Volkswirtschaft in Wort und Bild*, Special Supplement to the *Frankfurter Zeitung*, Frankfurt-am-Main, 1926; articles by Professor Bonn and Francis Delaisi, pp. iv to xii.

influential financial experts that the Dawes Scheme for German reparations will be inevitably revised in the course of the next five years, and that in connection with such a revision all previous agreements for the payment of inter-Allied debts will have to undergo a proportionate scaling down." It is well known that there is a section of opinion in the United States which has been working some time to encourage the idea of writing off a portion of the war debts owed by Europe to America. There can be no doubt that one of the difficulties in the way of this is the hasty agreement which was made in 1923 by Mr. Baldwin, whereby Great Britain bound herself down to the full sum without any consideration of the economic effect on the country. For this agreement was the prelude to the latest movement for deflation from which Britain has been suffering and is still suffering. But the task of those who are working for the scaling down of the international war debt in America is rendered more difficult by this Anglo-American debt agreement, for they are met with the reply that at least one country has already agreed to pay the full amount.

If the writing down of the international war debt may become a necessity at some future date, the tackling of the national or internal war debt problems has become even more urgent for the near future. In Germany the problem was solved by inflation on a scale unprecedented in history. A whole rentier class was ruined and the State freed from internal debt at the cost of the complete collapse of the home money market and general demoralization among all classes. On a smaller scale the lightening of the internal debt was effected by modified inflation in France. In Great Britain the converse monetary policy has resulted in an enormous increase in the internal debt, and a policy of drift has prevented any effort being made except by the minority members of the Colwyn Commission to deal with it. According to Mr. Ernest Bevin,[1] whereas before the war a British workman had to work twelve minutes every day to provide wealth for the holders of the internal debt, to-day he has to work an hour and three-quarters. The burden of debt in England to-day is such that it plays a big rôle in intensifying industrial depression. The high costs of production of British industry, relative to those countries which have practised inflation on the Continent, is largely due to the high charges in the form of taxation which the State has imposed on industry with the object of providing revenue to pay the £300 odd millions for the internal debt annually. Thus we can see the effect of the debt payment on prices, wages, and profits in industry by the following equation :—

$$M + W + I + P = V$$

where M = raw materials, W = wages, I = interest of internal debt, P = industrial profits, V = industrial prices. If I is increased, as is the case in England, by the war debt, and if V is decreased through a fall in prices resulting from monetary policy, then either W or P or M must be reduced. But in practice there is never a sufficient fall in prices to stabilize the equation except after a lapse of time. The price "lag" always is operative and the bulk of the burden falls on P and W. If, then, the banks deflate the currency while retaining a heavy internal debt, either industrial profits or wages suffer. In the case of Britain to-day, both have suffered, but, of course, the workers' wages most of all. Conversely, an income tax or capital levy to reduce debt would decrease I. Then if by monetary

[1] Speech at Labour Party Conference, Blackpool, October 6, 1927.

K

policy V was kept stable, W could be increased and the workers benefit. Monetary policy could be controlled in this manner under the following formula:—

$$\frac{C + B + D}{G} = V$$

where C = currency in circulation, B = bankers' credits, D = State debt, G = gold reserve, and V = industrial prices. A levy or tax to reduce debt would bring down D. This would bring down V or prices, and so cause deflation and intensify industrial depression. But this could be prevented by increasing B or bankers' credit. Thus a mild inflation of credit could counterbalance the deflationary effect of debt reduction. The alternative policy would be to expand C and B, to inflate currency by printing paper notes or increasing credit either to industry or to the workers by living wages and family allowances. This means that V at once increases, and if D or debt interest is fixed, then either W or P, or both, can increase. This means that wages and industrial profits rise. This is the usual phenomenon under inflation. But unfortunately its effect is only temporary. Inflation is always accompanied by a lack of confidence, people start to hoard materials (M), capital for investment becomes scarce, B decreases, C increases indefinitely, till finally D and B are wiped out and there is only left a paper currency C to balance against materials, wages, and profits. In other words, the whole system of banking and modern credit breaks down. Those who would ignore the problem of debt reduction by the gradual stages of levies and taxation, and only concern themselves with wage increases and family allowances, will certainly destroy the burden of debt, but will do so at the price of wrecking the whole credit system. This was the experience in Germany between 1919 and 1923. It was like burning down one's house in order to roast one's pig. On the other hand, a reduction of debt (D) accompanied by a rise in B and W will not upset the equation, and will maintain the whole fabric of banking credit (B), without which no modern community can very well function. Taxation of wealth should aim not only at increasing social services, but also at reducing debt, where the latter has become a serious burden on production, otherwise the balance of national economy is disturbed.

Our survey of the world debt problem, therefore, shows us the following picture. We see in the economic history of Europe since 1924 a tendency for the financial and banking interests centred in London and New York to take more direct control over industry and production in Europe than hitherto. For this purpose they have guaranteed extensive credits to European Governments to stabilize currency and to European industry to enable it to start out afresh on new developments, made possible by scientific discoveries. But in furthering this policy they are caught in the meshes of their own net which they laid when they imposed, cold-bloodedly, the full gold value of the war debts on the European Allies and the reparations payments on Germany. To get out of this difficulty they are trying various methods by way of extensive colonial developments, mainly in Eastern Europe, Asia, and South America, financed by the creditor nations and worked off in commodity exports to these areas by the debtors. How far this will succeed depends upon the solution of certain inherent contradictions which are within the capitalist system. But should these schemes fail, there is always a possibility of a scaling down of the reparations and debts to a figure which will minimize the contradictions in the present world economy. On a national scale in Britain a solution must be attempted by further taxation of wealth for debt reduction. The alternative of inflation has superficial attractions, but contains the seeds of as bad a disease as the one it is supposed to cure. In the absence of any national policy, the burden is left to press on industrial prosperity and on wages alike. The post-war financial system is trying to solve its problems and to liberate production, but a great deal depends upon whether it has the courage to face debt problems both nationally and internationally, and upon whether there are sufficient areas in the world which need development and the export of capital and goods to enable the economic system of Europe, so dangerously wounded in the World War, to recover from its wounds. The further possibility of colonial expansion for European and American capitalism in the post-war period we will consider in the next chapter.

CHAPTER XI

COLONIAL DEVELOPMENTS SINCE THE WAR—
POSSIBLE AND PROSPECTIVE

WE come now to consider the question whether in the present time there are sufficient colonial areas in the earth to provide markets for the manufactured goods of the highly industrialized States and sources of raw materials and areas for the investment of their surplus capital. This is without doubt the most serious problem which the captains of finance and industry in the world have got to solve. Unless they do solve it, the rapid accumulation of wealth in the United States will have no outlet, and will impinge upon the markets and investment areas of the older countries of Europe, and the latter will be unable to liquidate their obligations under the war debt agreements with the United States, let alone provide for the food and tropical produce which they must purchase every year, if they are to maintain the existing standard of living of their populations. The problem was hinted at by Mr. Garvin in the *Observer* as far back as August 23, 1925, when he wrote, apropos of the provisional Franco-British Debt Settlement: "The statesmen of the future in Britain, France, and Germany alike will have to strive to create between these three countries at least—not excluding Belgium and Italy—a system of economic co-operation bound to extend to the colonial sphere in tropical Africa at least."

We saw in earlier chapters how the export of capital to colonial areas is under modern economic conditions the usual forerunner of the export of commodities. The solution of the international debt problem, therefore, necessarily presupposes the export of capital either from the debtor States of Europe to undeveloped areas of the earth to develop the commodity exports, or from the chief creditor State, America, in order to facilitate the purchasing power of these colonies, whereby the latter can place orders on reparations account with the debtors. But apart from this, most of the European debtor States have to develop their exports either of commodities or of services in the form of capital, in order to pay for the needs of their ever-increasing populations, which cannot be fed and maintained on European produce alone. In the case of Great Britain, a foreign trade of about 30 per cent. of the total production of the country is carried on to pay for imports. How far all these imports are really needed is a matter which we will discuss in the next chapter. Having regard, however, to a necessary minimum which all highly industrialized countries must import, and having regard to the necessity for development of exports for war debt payments, it is natural that the search for investment fields and markets has become more and more keen since the war.

The United States has taken the lead over all countries in this respect, and the fact that she, least of all, requires capital exports, being largely self-sufficient, and, moreover, has no foreign debts to pay, makes her entry into the foreign investment field a still more serious matter for those for whom foreign investment is a most urgent matter. In 1913 the United States foreign investments were negligible and stood at about £500 millions. To-day they are about £2,600 millions, not counting £1,948 millions "political" investments in the form of war loans to the Allies. The direction into which this capital has gone may be surmised by an analysis of the capital issues for foreign investment in the United States.[1] Since 1924 it may be roughly said that this capital has gone in the following direction:—

Europe..	35 per cent.
Canada and North American Dominions ..	30 ,,
Southern and Central America	20 ,,
Asia	15 ,,

The movement of American capital to the North American Dominions had already begun before the war, and, as we have seen above, is largely taking the place of British capital which went there before. The same thing applies to Southern and Central America, except that British capital is still going there on a large scale, and the outlet seems so far to be sufficient for both. To Asia the United States has not as yet directed its fullest attention. In Europe the investment of capital is only since 1924, and has more the form of bondholders' capital invested in currency stabilization loans than of industrial capital invested in productive processes. We see, therefore, that the United States is a new factor to-day in the field of foreign investment and is already complicating the situation, in spite of its large home market, by competing in the areas of colonial development with those European countries which either by necessity, as debtors, or by reason of their large imports are bound to find constantly expanding markets for exports of goods and capital.

The most important of the countries in this category are Great Britain and Germany. The latter country's special problem, as chief debtor State of Europe under the Dawes reparation plan, has been dealt with in Chapter VIII. We will here consider the position

[1] See Dunn's *American Foreign Investments*. Viking Press, New York.

of Great Britain and the possibility of developing export markets for its goods and capital in the world to-day. It will be remembered that we examined the position of Great Britain in regard to capital export in a period before the war in Chapter IV. We came to the conclusion that the centre of gravity of British capital export was shifting from the North American continent and Europe to South America, Africa, and to Southern and Eastern Asia. Countries in what we called the C category, with large undeveloped areas but with growing native capital accumulation in industry, like Canada, were tending to provide more of their own capital requirements at home, and were thereby moving up into category B. The United States, which used to be a country of new capital accumulation and capital import in category B, has moved up into category A and become a country of old capital accumulation, self-supporting, and indeed capital exporting, as we have seen above. On the other hand, categories C, D, and E, undeveloped lands with little or no native commerce and industry, have been taking increasing quantities of British capital. Has this process continued since the war?

If we take British capital exports between the end of the war and 1925, we can arrive at certain tentative results, but it should be understood that exact figures are a matter of great difficulty to obtain. I have collected material from various sources, but I do not pretend to give more than a rough outline of the trend of British capital export since the war. Let us take the American continent first. The greatest change here took place in the relations between the United States and Great Britain. Whereas before the war Great Britain held £754 millions investments in the United States, during the war Great Britain financed her armies and her Allies partly by selling out her American securities, which were bought by Americans. In this way the United States set out on its career of becoming a creditor State. The securities sold by Great Britain during the war amounted to £284 millions.[1] In all probability the amount of British capital held in the United States is now somewhere about £470 millions. In Canada British investments have only increased by £2 millions since the war. Before the war Great Britain took 73 per cent. of Canada's loans; to-day she only takes 9 per cent. American capital is everywhere penetrating the country. The following figures of American and British investments in Canada have been kindly supplied me by Mr. J. T. Walton Newbold, and are extracted from the *Monetary Times of Canada*:—

YEAR 1923.

United States.	Great Britain.	Investment.
Dollars.	Dollars.	
701,000,000	456,000,000	Federal, Provincial, and City Loans
540,000,000	145,000,000	General Industries
370,000,000	745,000,000	Railways
325,000,000	60,000,000	Forests, Paper and Saw Mills
138,000,000	116,000,000	Public Utilities
50,000,000	100,000,000	Land
35,000,000	80,000,000	Banking and Insurance
25,000,000	85,000,000	Mortgages
235,000,000	100,000,000	Mining
6,000,000	3,000,000	Fisheries
2,425,000,000	1,890,000,000	

It is interesting to note here that the Americans are getting control by investment over the general industries, forests, mines, and fisheries of Canada, but that Great Britain still retains the lion's share of

[1] *Encyclopædia Britannica*, Supplement, p. 520.

the interest and control in the railways, land, banking, and insurance business. Taking it as a whole, however, Canada is not an area where Great Britain can look for a large export of capital, in view of the close proximity to the United States. Consequently the exports of British manufactured goods, of which under modern conditions capital export is the forerunner, is likely to find a limited outlet in Canada. Coming now to Central America, the United States Department of Commerce has estimated that British capital in Mexico amounts now to £164 millions and is still well ahead of American investments, which amount to £119 millions. This is an increase of £64 millions on 1913 and has mainly gone into railway, oil, and mining enterprises. The general inference is that Central America still offers to Great Britain a wide field for investment in mining industry of all kinds, with a market for the export of engineering machinery.

Coming now to South America, we find the following figures for British investments: Brazil, £285 millions, Argentine £410 millions, Chile £82 millions, Uruguay £41 millions.[1] For the whole of South America this is a rise of just over £100 millions on 1913, and a total for all South America of £818 millions. This corresponds with an estimate in a South American journal, *Latin America in 1927* (Dashwood House, E.C. 2), according to which the total in the South American continent is £1,105 millions, of which £270 millions are not earning anything. South America, in fact, continues to absorb an increasing quantity of British capital. The greater part of this is invested in railways which not only purchase their materials in England, and thereby open the way for export of goods, but also provide profits on the haulage of goods of all nations

[1] Report of the Bank of London and South America for the year 1926

in the South American republics. These profits are returned in bank balances to London and are classed as invisible exports. In addition to this there is the meat and grain trade of these republics, which are to a great extent in British hands and provide certain outlets for special machinery and pedigree livestock exports from Great Britain. In this connection it is interesting to note that recently American capital is coming to the Argentine in the form of fixed-interest bonds in State railways and public works. The major profits of these enterprises go to the Argentine people, while American capital gets mainly a fixed interest. In other words, the Argentine is going in for some practical socialism. British capital, on the other hand, is mainly of the type which takes all the risk and all the profit. As far as Brazil alone is concerned, there are vast tracts of prairies in the Upper Amazon valleys which will some day be available for agricultural produce and ranching economy, although a limit is probably placed to this by climatic conditions north of Tropic of Capricorn and by the difficulty of settling white populations there. South of this line the possibilities of European settlement are still far from exhausted, and economic developments with possibilities of large capital exports will be more rapid than north of this line, where European capital investment must go hand in hand with the increase of a native Indian class to provide unskilled labour. It is just this latter factor which in subtropical zones is the uncertain quantity and will make economic development in this part of South America slow. But of the possibilities of almost boundless development, both north and south of the line, either actual or potential, there can be no doubt. In the Amazon valley alone there are vast tracts of untouched forests and unused prairies which have never heard the sound of the locomotive whistle. European and American capitalism could find outlets for commodity export and capital investment for many decades ahead there. The chief difficulty is that owing to the factors mentioned above —labour and climate—the rate of opening up is likely to be slow and the economic system of Europe to-day requires immediate outlets.

Turning now to Asia, let us first consider the position of India as an outlet for British goods and capital since the war. It has been estimated from Indian sources that the amount of new British capital taken up in London for Indian industrial enterprises amounts to £38 millions between the end of the war and 1923. If we add to this the amounts invested in public debts since 1919, viz. £72 millions, we should reach a figure of about £110 millions, which, when added to the £450 millions of British capital invested there up to 1913, will bring the total to £560 millions. The amount is probably greater, and this is a conservative estimate. For instance, much of the capital issues in India to-day are really of British capital. Indeed, Sir M. Visvesvaraya, in his *Reconstructing India*, gives £411 millions as the figure for joint-stock companies registered in England and operating in India. The £238 millions British-held public debt would bring this to £642 millions. This figure is probably too high, and it is safer to take the lower one. But it is certainly true to suggest that there is no falling off of the rate at which India is being opened out by British capital, and the investment outlet seems to be unlimited. But if British capital continues to pour in there and along with native Indian capital to develop the country, the commodity exchange which results from Britain's capital exports to India has undergone considerable modification since the war. Formerly India used to receive large amounts of textile goods which went in direct exchange for Indian produce imported into England. Two-thirds of the Indian textile consumption used to be provided by Lancashire. To-day it is less than half, and the balance is supplied largely by native Indian and Japanese mills. A certain amount of British capital has gone into Indian textile mills, although how much is a matter for conjecture. British exports to India are becoming more and more constructional in kind and less of the type to be consumed. Thus engineering goods and technical equipment of all kinds replace to some extent exports of textile goods. But in addition to this the tendency is for Britain's trade with India to become passive, which seems to suggest that India is paying her interest on the British capital invested there by increasing her imports of food and raw material into Britain without any corresponding exchange of commodities. Still, whether Great Britain becomes more and more a mere banker to Indian industries, and less and less a workshop supplying her with technical requirements, the fact seems to remain that the outlet for capital investment in India is still very great and shows no sign of diminishing. Moreover, new industries springing up in England, to which I shall refer later, will undoubtedly be able to redress somewhat the tendency for Britain's textile exports to India to decrease.

Coming to China, we find again a large increase in capital exports. In 1926 the Chinese Government Bonds issued in London amounted to £27 millions and railway stocks to £15 millions, while unsecured bonds amounted to £3 millions odd, making a total of £45 millions. British shipping and commercial interests in the Yang-tse Valley alone were estimated in 1926 to amount to about £200 millions. The *Financial Times* in the same year estimated the total value of British capital invested in China at about £300 millions, which would allow on the previous reckoning about £50 millions in private business, banking, and commercial interests in China outside the Yang-tse Valley. The figures are admittedly rough, but there are enough to show that British capital exports since the war have increased by over £90 millions. The British Chamber of Commerce at Shanghai made in 1927 an estimate at a round figure of £350 millions. In any case it is clear that there is still an enormous field in China, and the position is to some extent similar to that in India. For in China British consumption goods are tending to decline and to be replaced by invisible exports. The cause of the decline, however, is not so much the competition of native and Japanese mills as the direct political, anti-British boycott. The Chinese revolutionary movement, supported not only by the intellectual and peasant classes of China but also by the business and commercial interests, is resenting the monopolistic rights which the British have acquired in the course of decades in the South of China. It is trying to secure better terms from the capitalists of other nations, notably the United States, whose Chinese policy has been much more accommodating to the Chinese revolutionary national movement than the British. Undoubtedly, if the British Government followed a more conciliatory Chinese policy, the outlet for British commodity exports, as well as for capital, would be greater than it is to-day. The 400 million Chinese live under conditions of extreme poverty and with a low standard of life. A raising of that standard, which the revolutionary elements are aiming at, would make possible a large increase of the effective demand for consumption goods in which the textile industry of Lancashire could share, while the opening up of the country with railways and public works would provide a large outlet for the exports of British metallurgical industry. As things are at present the tendency seems to be, as in India, for Britain to receive Chinese food products and raw material in exchange largely for banking, insurance, shipping, and other invisible exports.

In Japan an increase of something like £30 million British investments of capital seems to have taken place since the war. This is largely accounted for by the big 1924 Japanese Government loan of £25 millions to replace the damage of the earthquake. This, together with small increases in business investment in Japan, brings the total British capital there to the neighbourhood of £100 millions. The outlet here is somewhat limited, because the growth of Japanese capital accumulation leaves little room for outside capital, and, indeed, the Japanese capitalists are investing large sums of money abroad themselves, largely in Manchuria. It is estimated that £120 millions have gone there already.[1]

In the East Indies—that is, the Federated Malay States, Siam, Burma, and the Dutch Indies—a very large potential field is now being developed for British capital and commodity exports. Taking all these areas together, it seems that a total amount of £130 millions has gone there since the war. In the Federated Malay States £17 millions are now invested in Government and municipal bonds, £2¾ millions in tin, £3 millions in hydro-electric enterprises, and £22 millions in railways. This makes a total of £44¾ millions. In 1925 the rubber boom accounted for a large increase in investments in rubber plantations, for the British and the Dutch planters now supply the bulk of the world's rubber. £150 millions can now be estimated as being invested in the rubber industry in the Malay States and £16 millions in the tin industry in that

[1] *The Times* Peking correspondence, August 25, 1927.

country, Siam, and Burma. There is probably another
£50 millions in the Dutch Indies invested in rubber.
This would bring the total British capital in the British
and Dutch Indies to £250 millions. In the Philippines, British capital still takes the lead over American
and is estimated at about £50 millions.[1] The prospects
of a developing market for capital and commodities
in South-East Asia are undoubtedly great for many
years to come. This area of the world produces the
bulk of the world's rubber and tin supplies, two
commodities of prime necessity for mankind, and a
large part of the sources of supply lie within the
British Empire. The exploitation of these raw materials
will absorb for a long time to come a good deal of
British capital, besides providing a moderate and
expanding market for equipment of all kinds.

Australia has become one of the most inveterate
borrowers of capital from the Mother Country since
the war. But she is a country which has developed
into the B category and is now beginning to supply
some of her own local needs of capital. British investors
are becoming more and more of the bondholder type,
holding Government, municipal, and State railway
bonds, for the Australian Governments are developing
a sound and practical socialistic sense, and are tending
to let foreign capital mainly into the fixed-interest-
bearing type of investment, reserving the larger share
of the profits for the community, by State ownership
of public services. British capital invested in Australian
Commonwealth and State debt, bonds, and public
utility companies amounted to about £492 millions
in 1925—an increase of about £56 millions on pre-war.
There has been some discussion recently on the financial
stability of Australia, in view of the large amounts
which she has borrowed, not altogether for productive

[1] Dunn's *American Foreign Investments*.

purposes, and this, combined with the fact that she is borrowing mainly the low-interest-bearing bondholder type of capital, seems to suggest that the stream of British capital investments thither is not likely to go on increasing so fast. As regards outlets for commodity exports, there is every probability of a gradual increase of the most highly finished wares, but not of the products of cheap mass production, which will be increasingly supplied by native capitalists.

On the African continent it is necessary to distinguish three areas of investment, the Dominion of South Africa, the Crown Colonies, Egypt and the Sudan. The first comes under the C category of country.[1] Along with Canada, the Argentine, and Australia, the Union of South Africa is developing native industry, but has still large needs for capital for development from outside. Unlike Canada, however, this new capital is not being mainly provided by the United States, and the British money market is still the principal source from which the Union of South Africa draws. Thus it appears that the sum of £46 millions has been borrowed by the Government of the Union in London between 1913 and March 1925.[2] The other great investment field in South Africa is mines. According to the report of the Transvaal Chamber of Mines,[3] the increased capital absorbed by the South African mines between 1913 and 1926 was £41 millions. The total British capital in the mines in 1925 is estimated at £32 millions, as against £22 millions in 1913—an increase of £10 millions. Land and other forms of enterprise have probably absorbed

[1] See Chapter IV.
[2] See Report on Resumption of Gold Payments by the Union of South Africa. Government Printing Office, Pretoria, 1925, Annexe 12.
[3] Gold Producers' Committee, Arbitration Report, 1926–1927, p. 117.

another £5 millions at least, which would bring the total to about £61 millions. We estimated [1] British capital in 1913 in South Africa at about £380 millions, which on this calculation would be brought up to £441 millions for 1926.

The next two areas of colonial development in Africa fall under category D, and comprise Egypt and the Sudan and the East African Crown Colonies. In these areas native commerce alone is developed and industrial and finance capital is almost entirely supplied from Europe, with the possible exception of Egypt, which is qualifying rapidly for the C category with native industrial accumulations of capital. From one source it has been estimated that £65 millions of British capital are invested in Egypt and the Sudan, of which £48 millions are in Government loans, £7 millions in canals and docks, £3 millions in railways, and £4 millions in banks. This is certainly an underestimate, for very large sums of money have been invested in irrigation works and in electric light and power development in the Sudan, in which Dorman Long & Co., the English Electric Co., and the Prudential Insurance Co. are interested. It would probably be nearer the mark to put the total British capital in Egypt and the Sudan at £100 millions. As regards the East African Crown Colonies—Kenya, Tanganyika, and Uganda—the amount of Government loans subscribed in London up to 1925 amounted to £24 millions, while British industrial concerns operating in these territories have a combined capital of £15 millions, making the total about £39 millions. [2] The Crown Colonies on the West Coast of Africa belong to the E category, because the natives there are largely in

[1] Chapter IV.
[2] *British Imperialism in East Africa*, Colonial Series No. 1, published by the Labour Research Department, London, 1927.

the tribal state. The principal industrial developments undertaken by the British are in Nigeria, where
a railway loan of £12 millions is projected and partly
taken up. On the Gold Coast a £4 million loan was
taken up in 1920. Considerable sums are invested
there in tin and in the palm-oil industry, and it would
probably be not far wrong to estimate British capital
investments in Nigeria, the Gold Coast, and Sierra
Leone at £25 millions.[1]

This brings the total of British capital in the African
continent to about £605 millions—a rise of £75 millions
on the 1913 figures—of which £61 millions went to the
South African Union and £14 millions to the rest of
British Africa. This indicates a steady flow of investment into Africa, faster in the Dominion of South Africa
than in the, as yet, primitive tropical areas. Undoubtedly
Africa is one of the most promising colonial areas
in the world for restoring the weakened industrial
economy of Europe. Its types of climate are very
varied. In the south there are large territories which
have been, and still are, being settled by white men,
and afford opportunities for immigration. There are
also considerable territories in tropical Africa above
a certain altitude where the white man can settle,
especially in Kenya, Uganda, and Tanganyika. The
tableland of Africa rises with great regularity from
the seaboard to the heart of the continent, where great
tropical forests exist. The white man's country lies
in belts between the seaboard and the tropical forests.
But almost more important for the economy of Europe
is the prospect of economic development in the areas

[1] According to the *Nigerian Tin Handbook* (Mining Publication
Committee, Salisbury House, London, 1927), the issued capital
of British tin companies registered in London and operating in
Nigeria was £2½ millions in 1913, and £5 millions in 1926, showing
that £2½ millions of British capital had gone into tin in Nigeria during
this period.

where the white man is merely there as an administrator, engineer, and foreman. Here the native black population live mostly under the tribal system, as agriculturists. Their standard of living is very low from a European standpoint, but the population of the vast continent is so great that even a small rise in its consuming power would have a tremendous effect on European exports of manufactured articles. The introduction of better methods of cultivation and the construction of roads would revolutionize the life of the native and raise the demand for bicycles and agricultural implements, which only Europe could supply, because Africa is without coal and iron deposits and so is unlikely under the present industrial condition prevailing in the world to develop large industries in competition with Europe. The construction of railways also is having a tremendous effect in raising the import and export trade of tropical Africa. The coming of the railway to Kano, in Nigeria, raised the export of ground-nuts from nil to 120,000 tons in 1925. This was largely made possible by the reduction in transport charges. In the cotton-growing district of Zaria, in Nigeria, the railway reduced transport charges from 3s. per ton-mile to $1\frac{1}{2}$d. per ton-mile. Railway construction in Kenya and Uganda has raised the exports of these areas from £$2\frac{1}{4}$ millions in 1921 to £$7\frac{3}{4}$ millions in 1925, and of the Gold Coast from £6 millions in 1921 to £$10\frac{1}{2}$ millions in 1925. Imports from Europe to the tropical African colonies are in some cases greater than exports to Europe, and indicate that the capital investments from Europe are being used to open up the agricultural production of the continent. The principal way in which this is done is by the construction of railways and roads to feed them with European materials imported to Africa, and the interest on the capital thus lent will be repaid in later years in palm-nuts, cotton, cocoa, and other tropical produce. Potentially there seems no limit to the development which can go on on these lines.

But human and social factors are at work which make the rate of development slow, and may endanger the outlet for European capital and goods, if not dealt with in time. In those British Crown Colonies of tropical Africa where white settlers can take up land and farm, the native tribes and tribal customs are being ruthlessly broken down, the natives deprived of their land and confined to inadequate "reserves," while the best territories are being taken for the settlers. The white settler is trying to reduce the native from being an independent agriculturist to a "wage-slave" in the literal sense of the word. The European capitalist is not content to leave it to the natural tendencies of the native to expand his wants and to come and work for a part of the year on his plantations for wages with which he can then buy a few luxuries. He chafes at the native longing to go back to his land and restrict his wants to modest proportions. He is, therefore, in favour of a policy of depriving the native of his immemorial rights to the land of his fathers, imposing head and poll taxes on him, which he can only liquidate by going to work for wages. Sooner or later this policy, if allowed to go on unchecked, must lead either to grave political unrest among the natives or more probably to a physical degeneration of the native population and its ultimate dying out. For the African native is of the type which will stubbornly resist social innovations imposed from without even to the extent of racial suicide. Already contact with European civilization in the coastal towns has brought about degeneration of the native, the spread of European diseases, and a tendency for the population to decrease. Indeed, it is very questionable if there has been any increase in the native population of Africa as a whole since the white man took over the continent. If this tendency is to remain unchecked, there will be an end to the prospect of Africa becoming the outlet for capital and commodities for Europe which it promises to be to-day.

On the other hand, British administrators in Africa seem to be aware of the danger which the unrestrained predatory capitalism of the European planter and concessionaire would like to drive Africa into. Thus the Senior Commissioner for Tanganyika, Major Orde Brown, writes in 1926,[1] defending the condition of Tanganyika, where the native rights are much better protected than in the neighbouring Kenya: "The impact of the capitalistic system upon the African social organization in Tanganyika has not the dangers that it would have elsewhere; the almost entire absence of any class earning a living by industrial crafts eliminates the tragedy of the gradual crushing of such a class by mechanical competition. . . . The class sometimes termed 'wage-slaves' is non-existent in Tanganyika." Similarly, the Hon. W. Ormsby Gore, in an address to the Geographical Section of the British Association, in 1926, said: "The creation of large industrial centres in tropical Africa, with workers completely divorced from food production, would be an entire innovation of very doubtful desirability. The African man is firmly attached to the soil, and the whole fabric of social organization is built upon the right to cultivate." He added that the European man had four duties in Africa: firstly, to combat African diseases and to raise the native's standard of health; secondly, to improve the methods of native cultivation; thirdly, to construct railways and roads; and fourthly, to give the native an education which

[1] Colonial Paper No. 19, H.M. Stationery Office.

will not merely make him a bad imitation of a European, but will rather tend to develop his individuality and his personal independence.

It may be said in conclusion that the possibilities of debt-ridden and industrially depressed Europe reviving itself economically by the development of Africa are almost boundless. As the Hon. W. Ormsby Gore said in the address quoted above, "Tropical Africa is a natural new market for the manufactured goods of the temperate zones, and between tropical Africa and the countries inhabited by Europeans there is a natural complementary trade between raw materials and food-stuffs of the one and the manufactured goods of the other." But the absolute condition of this development is the absence of predatory capitalistic exploitation of the African native and a sympathetic attitude towards the native social problem.

Coming now to the last area of capital export for Britain, we find an important outlet in Europe itself, which has developed since the war. The £103 millions lent to pre-revolutionary Russia must be regarded as written off as a bad debt. On the other hand, since the stabilization of European currencies a considerable amount of investment of British capital has been going on along with American capital in Europe. This has mainly taken the form of Government loans, partly for currency purposes and partly for general after-war reconstruction. Since 1921 loans have been raised in London by Czecho-Slovakia (£3 millions), Germany (Dawes Loan, £11 millions), Austria (£13 millions), Greece (Refugee and Reconstruction Loan, £9 millions), Hungary (Currency Stabilization and Debt Funding Loans, £7½ millions), Rumania (£17 millions), Scandinavian countries (£3 millions), making a total of £63 millions up to September 1926. It cannot be said that much of this capital raised will

increase the productive resources of Europe. Its
main result will be to repair war damages and provide
working capital for countries which lost that capital
in the post-war inflation wave. Further capital invested
by Britain in industries on the Continent since the war
has taken the form of oil development in the Carpathians and Rumania, commercial banking in Austria-
Hungary and Czecho-Slovakia, shipping interests on
the Danube, sugar financing in Poland. Then there
are short-term industrial credits which have been
given in considerable quantities along with American
credits to German industries, but they have been to
some extent repaid, and how much of them is out-
standing is difficult to estimate. The probability is
that the increase of British capital on the continent of
Europe since the war amounts to about £90 millions,
which would bring the total to £274 millions. This
is, after Asia and South America, the largest increase
in capital export since 1913. But, as I have shown
above, it is less healthy than the smaller increase of
capital export in Africa. On the other hand, there are
large areas of Europe that are waiting for development, and in the work of which British capital and
industry could have a share. Even excluding Russia,
there is an area on the middle Danube and along the
reaches of the Vistula, and lying between the Adriatic
on the south and the Baltic and Black Sea on the
north and east, which is peopled by 80 million people,
mainly peasants, with primitive domestic economy.
If the black earth lands which these peasants cultivate
in Hungary, Rumania, Yugoslavia, and Galicia could
be cultivated by modern methods, if the water power
of the Carpathians were fully developed and the forest
products of the Balkans brought by transport to the
sea, there would be abundant work for idle factories in
Great Britain providing the equipment for this develop-

ment work. But it seems that this area of the world is going to be left, by the financial and industrial heads in Britain, for Germany, as an area in which she may work off her reparation debts. As far as Russia is concerned this consideration possibly also applies, as well as the political fears of the British ruling class and the sulkiness of the holders of Tsarist bonds in the City, who are ruining a great outlet for British trade and capital by their short-sighted Shylock policy.

Tabulating, therefore, the figures for British capital investment since the war, and comparing them with the figures for 1913, the result is as shown in the table on p. 170.

We see from the table that there has been no real change in the direction of British capital exports since the war. The same tendencies which were operating then operate now. The war seems only to have intensified the process, but not to have altered its nature. There has been a still further reduction of the amount of investments held in the North American continent, due to the indebtedness to the United States and to the latter's penetration of Canada. On the other hand, capital export to South America holds the next position after the Malay States, East Indies, and India, which still hold the first place. Eastern and Southern Asia generally are the principal investment areas of the British Empire. After South America comes Europe, but this area must be to some extent discounted, as being only partly of a productive type. Next comes Central America and then Africa, which probably holds the greatest potentialities of any part of the world, though the present rate of investment is not high.

It will be observed that of the eight investment areas in which the increase of capital export has been over

(In millions sterling.)

	1913.	1926.	Increase over 1913.	Priority of Increase.
AMERICAN CONTINENT—				
Mexico	100	164	+ 64	6
Canada	376	378	+ 2	12
United States	754	470	− 284	13
Argentine	477	410		
Brazil		285		
Other South American Republics	238	123		
	715	818	+ 103	3
	1,945	1,830		
ASIATIC CONTINENT—				
India	450	560	+ 110	2
China	208	300	+ 92	4
East Indies, Malaya, etc.	120	250	+ 130	1
Japan	70	100	+ 30	9
Philippines	40	50	+ 10	11
	888	1,260		
AUSTRALASIA	436	492	+ 56	8
AFRICAN CONTINENT—				
Union of South Africa	380	441	+ 61	7
Egypt and Sudan		100		
African Crown Colonies		39		
W.A. Crown Colonies		25		
African Crown Colonies	150	164	+ 14	10
	530	605		
EUROPE—				
Russia	103	Nil		
Rest of Europe	81	274	+ 90	5
	184	274		
Total	£3,983	£4,461	£478	

£50 millions since 1913, four are outside the British Empire and yield a total increase of capital export of £349 millions. The remaining four are within the British Empire and provide a total increase of capital export of £357 millions. Although it must be noted that one country, India, within the Empire provides, with the Malay States and East Indies, the greatest investment area of any, namely, £240 millions since 1913, the actual value of South America, Central America, China, and Europe as an investment field, and consequently as a potential commodity market, is quite as great in the aggregate as are the chief capital markets of the British Empire. This only serves to emphasize the saying which I quoted in an earlier chapter as typical of contemporary world economy, viz. that trade does not necessarily follow the flag, but it does follow the cash.

Finally, it transpires from this survey that only a sympathetic attitude towards the native national movements in Asia and the colour problem in Africa will ensure for Great Britain any substantial share of the export trade and developments requiring capital in those colonial areas of the world. We have seen above that they are the most promising areas of any, but unless their social and political problems are solved, the economic advantage will not accrue to Great Britain. In South Africa the Dominion Government will tolerate no interference in these problems, but in the Crown Colonies, in India, and China, Great Britain has her fate in her own hands.

CHAPTER XII

THE NEW INDUSTRIAL REVOLUTION AND THE HOME MARKET

THE review of the colonial markets in the last chapter does not seem to suggest any catastrophic crisis confronting the West European economic systems, owing to an absence of expanding possibilities for capital and commodity export. All that can be said is that certain tendencies, already noticeable before the war, have become still more pronounced since. In the United States the tendency is to expand capital exports in the North and South American continent and in Europe. In Great Britain the expansion is mainly in South America, Eastern and Southern Asia, and Africa. The war seems only to have intensified a tendency already existing. On the other hand, the rate of capital export has increased enormously in the United States and decreased in Great Britain. The United States before the war was in debt to the world by at least £500 millions, and in 1926 was owed by the world £2,500 millions commercial debt and £1,948 millions political war debts. Great Britain, on the other hand, had increased her foreign credit at a much slower rate. She was owed by the world £3,192 millions in 1910, £4,000 millions in 1913, and £4,360 millions in 1925, in addition to a "political" or war debt of £1,817. Thus while Great Britain is still the largest lender in the world, she is fast being caught up by the United States, for her rate of increase of foreign investments is decidedly slowing down. In addition to this she has a debt of £900 millions to the United States, contracted during the war, and a sixfold increase in her internal debt. The investigations of Professor Bowley and Sir Josiah Stamp [1] tend to show (1) that Britain's income from home industries and investments has kept pace with the growth of population, (2) that her income from foreign investments has fallen, through the fact that the rate of increase of foreign investment is less than the increase of foreign indebtedness due to the American war debt. Moreover, the rise of national and other movements in the colonial parts of the earth has restricted the operations of foreign, and particularly British, capital abroad. The national movement in China is responsible for the boycott of British goods, and native capital in India and in the self-governing dominions is to some extent replacing that of the Mother Country. Another very important factor is Russia, which covers one-sixth of the earth's surface and is an enormous potential field of investment. This is now virtually closed to foreign capital. The Soviet State is trying to accumulate economic values from its own peasantry and from its nationalized industries, but the rate of accumulation is slow. Thus according to Soviet sources the pre-war national savings of Russia used to accumulate at the rate of £113 millions a year, largely in private hands. In 1924 only £51 millions were saved for national investment, of which £21 millions accumulated in the hands of the State and £30 millions in private hands. A lot depends on whether the Soviet leaders are able to raise their rate of accumulation of savings and so dispense with the necessity of calling on foreign capital to assist them. If the latter should prove to be the case, Western Europe will ultimately lose Russia as an investment area, though even so Russia will have to pass through a difficult transition period

[1] *The National Income*, 1924. Clarendon Press.

before her national savings reach the normal. But the probability is that Russia, even with her nationalized key industries working at full swing, will require foreign capital for decades to come. At present her rate of accumulation can hardly do more than replace the wear and tear of old industrial plant. Thus it is clear how mistaken a policy it is for Great Britain to cut herself off from the Russian market for capital and commodities out of political considerations, when all such openings are needed to balance the national income and expenditure. This balance is much more difficult to effect now, in view of colonial national movements and American war debt, than was the case before the war.

On the other hand, there is no evidence of an economic breakdown in the national economy of Britain. The national income is estimated at £4,213 millions a year [1] and the wages bill at £1,600 millions, which is 44 per cent. of the national income, as against 43 per cent. in 1911. Against this there is an unemployment and short-time burden which lowers the income of sections of the working class. But against this there is roughly £300 millions which is spent on social services, which were not spent in 1911, and on balance the average position of the working classes is not worse than it was before the war; some may be worse, but others better off. There is reason to believe that, while the workers get roughly the same real values from the national income, the amount left over as a surplus for luxury expenditure and savings for investment is less than before the war. As far as the former item is concerned, that is all to the good, but it is not without importance in its bearing on the savings for investment in industry. The amount taken in taxation for war debt and for

[1] Professor Bowley and Sir Josiah Stamp, *op. cit.*

the £300 millions extra for social services, desirable
as the latter expenditure is, probably has the effect
of leaving less for investment in industry at home
and abroad. Moreover, while the total real income is
the same as before the war, the population has risen
7 per cent., so that the national income per head is
down some 5 per cent. Under the circumstances it is
not surprising to find that, whereas the annual national
saving was 16 per cent. of the total income in 1913,
it was only 12 per cent. in 1924.

It is interesting to know how that part of the
saving, which is not spent on luxury, is invested.
The following table is compiled from figures given
in the *Economist*, and contains the total figures for
British investments at home and abroad from 1913
to 1926:—

(In millions sterling.)

	1912.	1913.	1923.	1924.	1925.	1926.	Average for two Pre-war Years.	Average for five Post-war Years.
Total savings invested	210	196	271	209	232	230	203	235
Amount invested at home ..	45	35	133	84	155	129	40	125
Amount invested abroad ..	164	160	137	124	77	101	162	109

One may make three deductions from these
figures:—

(1) The total saved for investment from 1923 to
1926 is on an average £32 millions above the
figure for the last two pre-war years, but £29 millions less if the former are reduced to 1913 money
values.

(2) The amount invested at home from 1923 to 1926 is on an average £81 millions more than the average for the last two pre-war years and £50 millions a year more if reckoned in 1913 money values.

(3) The amount invested abroad between 1923 and 1926 is on an average £50 millions a year less than the average of the last two pre-war years; and £80 millions a year less when reckoned in 1913 values.

The tendency, therefore, is clearly seen to increase investments in home industry, and to reduce the rate of foreign investments. This bears out the evidence in former chapters.

In view of the drop in total national savings it is pertinent to ask if we are even now investing too much abroad. Mr. J. M. Keynes suggests [1] that we should invest abroad not more than £75 millions a year instead of the average of £109 millions, as we have done during the last five years. But if we are over-investing abroad, the result ought to make itself felt in a fall of the dollar-sterling exchange. In actual fact the reverse has been the case during the last three years. This may, however, be due to other factors coming in, such as the increase of American short-term loans to the London money market, enabling Britain to borrow "short" and lend "long." If this is the case, a dangerous element is introduced into the situation, for a crisis in the United States or a boom on the home market there might withdraw large amounts of money, lent now on short term to London and used by London to lend on long term at a higher rate elsewhere. There can be no doubt that America's financial return to Europe is not only supporting the European exchanges, but might enable the European money markets to lend abroad more than these markets could afford to lend if left to their own resources. On the other hand, it

[1] *The Nation*, February 12, 1927.

may be that that part of the national income derived from foreign investment is under-estimated, and that we can afford to re-invest abroad more than the £75 millions proposed by Mr. Keynes. Our income from foreign resources is estimated by Bowley and Stamp [1] at £156 millions in 1926, as against £194 millions in 1913. Now £156 millions represents £117 millions in 1913 values, which means that we now draw considerably less in real value from foreign investments than before the war. But £156 millions may be too small a figure, if we take the amount of £4,461 millions as representing the capital value of British foreign investments arrived at in Chapter X. Now 5 per cent. on this would mean an income of £223 millions from foreign sources. Against this there would have to be a deduction for the American debt payments, but even so the figure would be about £20 millions more than the Bowley and Stamp estimate. It is significant also to note that the Board of Trade has revised its estimate of Britain's invisible exports twice in recent years, and both times in an upward direction. Moreover, there are items of foreign income which are difficult to estimate. For instance, we do not know how much foreign debt is repaid to British investors each year from abroad and re-lent in larger amounts. We do not know what fresh capital issues in the form of bonus shares to existing holders in Britain are made annually by foreign companies. These amounts, if considerable, would tend to swell that portion of the national income which comes from abroad. But until we have more statistical information we can only guess at the position, and one of the most urgent problems before the country now is the eliciting of information on this subject. The joint-stock banks and the Bank of England are the only institutions

[1] *Op. cit.*

M

which could help in this matter of collecting information, and it is to be hoped that their chairmen and
governors will enlighten the public soon on these
subjects.

One fact emerges from the above, namely, the fall
in real values received from foreign investments
since the war. This is probably not an unmixed
blessing, for it may force more concentration on home
production and on the home market. It is an axiom
of the system of private ownership of capital that
profits of production after payment of raw material
and labour are re-invested wherever the highest
interest on capital is obtainable. Thus one of the causes
of the decline in gilt-edged securities before the war
was the competition of higher-yielding securities
abroad in young colonial countries, where capital
was scarce, the demand great and profits relatively
high. Capital always flows to where it gets the highest
interest, as long as everything is left to the unregulated
law of supply and demand. Interference in the field
of investment is difficult to undertake in a country
where private enterprise is unrestricted. It may,
therefore, come about that the decline in opportunities
for investment abroad at the same rate as formerly
may bring the interest rates for foreign investments
gradually nearer to the level prevailing at home.
The attraction of capital export would therefore not
be so great, and more would tend to flow into the
home money market. There is, no doubt, a move in
this direction going on to-day, as the figures for
capital applications in recent years seem to suggest. The
closer approximation of the rate of interest on capital
in Great Britain and in, let us say, the dominions,
is due partly to the increasing stability of those
dominions and the passing of the pioneer stage of
high interest, and partly also to the rise of interest

rates in Great Britain due to the war and the large Government war loans at interest rates 1 to 1½ per cent. above the pre-war level. Whether interest rates will fall in the future depends partly on Government financial policy and the extent to which efforts are made to reduce the National Debt by taxation or levies for the sinking fund and partly by the amount of gold and credit or investment capital which America sends to Europe. If America continues to lend abroad at the present rate, money rates should lower. On the other hand, the present policy of drift in regard to the National Debt of Great Britain is not likely to inspire confidence of the money market or lead to lower rates of interest, so much needed for home industrial developments. But a higher sinking fund, combined with a reduction in the rate of foreign investment, would tend to cheapen money at home and facilitate development of the national resources of Great Britain. A Government inspired with a sense of its social responsibility to the people, rather than to the moneyed interests, would assist this process by administrative and even legislative measures. Already in 1925 the " City " placed a restriction on the amount of foreign issues on the London money market, and there is no reason why Government should not assist the process of diverting capital to where it will be of the greatest use to the public. For to-day it is a sounder policy to accept a reduction of our export trade and foreign investments and concentrate on raising the efficiency of our production and standard of living at home.

It would be, of course, disastrous to ignore the need for foreign investments, if they take the form of "invisible exports" to pay for imports of food and raw material of industry. Without this, Great Britain cannot live, and there is no use fostering the illusion that a 45-million population, the greater part of which is industrial, can grow all its own food, let alone provide the tropical products without which the standard of living of the people would be seriously reduced. The mild, humid climate of Britain is not conducive, over a large part of it, to the production of cereals, and the tendency since the eighties of last century to concentrate on stock-raising is the result of these natural conditions. Moreover, the raw material of the textile trade of Lancashire and the oils for the soap and chemical industries, rubber and certain metals, can only be grown or obtained in tropical or subtropical countries. Again, the seeds for feeding-stuffs for cattle can be produced in African velds and Manchurian prairies far cheaper than their equivalents in calorie value can be produced in England. It would therefore be madness to imagine that we can neglect the problem of how to pay by export of commodities or capital investment for these necessary products. At present some 25 per cent. of the total British production is destined for foreign markets, and this, with invisible exports, pays for imports and for the American debt.

On the other hand, there may be some reason for thinking that some of the articles which are imported are not strictly needed for the national economy. The figures of the imports into the United Kingdom, as issued by the Board of Trade, but regrouped under various headings, show us ways which may be explored in this connection.

They show us that certain important items of food and raw material, upon which the existence of the country depends, could not be cut down under any circumstances. Thus in 1926 the £99 millions odd for grains and flour, £114 millions for meat, £84 millions for raw cotton, £65 millions for raw wool,

£45 millions for oils and seeds, £43 millions for oils and fats, either cannot be produced at all in the sub-temperate climate of Britain or else cannot be produced in sufficient quantities to support the existing population. On the other hand, there are other items which do not necessarily come under the category of necessities. There are £275 millions for "Other Food and Drink," which represents a truly enormous figure, and while a large part of this may quite well be essential to national well-being, there is more than a suspicion that a portion represents luxury articles which could at a pinch be done without if it were a question of reducing the total imports. The same applies to £31 millions of "Other Textile Manufactures," £17 millions for "Apparel," and £64 millions for "Other Manufactured Goods." It is possible also that in the more distant future a portion of the £39 millions for timber could be done without if a policy of national afforestation were carried out on a large scale, as is possible on some lands in the North of England and Scotland. The fuel-oil bill might also be reduced by distilling oils from coal, upon which scientific research has been active in recent years. That a reduction of imports could be effected to the tune of some £50 millions a year by curtailing unnecessary luxuries is quite within the bounds of possibility, and this would reduce the urgency of the export problem by that amount. On the other hand, it must be noted that the great bulk of British imports, running into roughly one and three-quarter thousand millions a year, are indispensable to the national economy. Nevertheless it may become necessary to develop taxation of luxuries and to devise some method of regulating imports under the quota system by National Import Boards, which, while not subjecting trade to the uncertainties and injustices of tariffs, would establish a maximum import of certain items for each year. This was done in the war, and its effects on the general trade of the country would be advantageous by tending towards price stabilization and by enabling both agriculturist, industrialist, and labourer to know where he is.

In addition to certain superfluous imports which might be cut down and thereby reduce somewhat the need for increasing foreign markets, there is room to examine the possibilities of reducing exports of capital which may not be strictly fulfilling their legitimate object. Under a socialized system of banking and investment the amount of capital for which the public would be asked to subscribe would bear strict relation to the public utility of the concerns needing the new capital. The Stock Exchange Committee would only open subscription lists for enterprises which it was satisfied were engaged in productive enterprise, such as in constructing railways in undeveloped lands, providing conveniences which are calculated to raise the purchasing power of the community. There would be some rough sort of connection between the amount of capital which goes to "constructional" goods, like railways and docks on the one hand, and the amount that goes to "consumption" goods, such as perishable commodities, on the other. It was on just this failure to observe a balance between the production of these two kinds of goods that Karl Marx based his masterly criticism of private capitalism in his second volume of *Capital*, chapter xxi. For, as it is at present, large sums are raised every year from the public on the money market which go to quite unproductive objects. Thus in the last half-year of 1926 there was raised on the London Stock Exchange over £91 millions of new capital for purposes both at home and abroad (reckoning in only those companies with a capital of £1 million and over). Of this, £72 millions were devoted to reconstructing old companies, shuffling shares of existing concerns, and generally inflating capital without any corresponding increase in the productive capacity of the companies concerned! In the rubber boom of 1925 large sums of capital were raised for foreign investment on this basis, and whenever there is a boom in foreign mines a large amount of capital is subscribed in Britain and exported which might just as well stay at home, as it is only enriching the speculators and company promoters who are floating new concerns, issuing new capital, and not increasing the wealth of the world at large.

Thus it appears that we are buying from abroad a certain number of articles which we do not really need for our national economy, and are sending abroad some capital which is not earning a satisfactory return, because it is of the so-called "watered" type. We could, in other words, be more economical in the things we buy and more careful in our methods of payment.

This brings us to the problem of making capital, which under unrestricted private initiative always runs after the highest interest, move into channels where it may earn less, but will nevertheless produce more actual real wealth for the mass of the nation. It is hardly likely to do this without compulsion, either in the form of special taxation or of restriction on certain types of foreign investment by a State control of banking operations. Private capital will not go into home electricity development schemes, or into sugar factories to work up the produce of British agriculture at 6 per cent. or 7 per cent., when it can get 8 per cent. and 9 per cent. and various pickings and commissions by floating a reconstruction loan of some speculative finance company in Rhodesia. Not that foreign investment and colonial developments are not wanted, but there is a limit to what the country can afford. Surplus national savings ought to be encouraged and at a pinch compelled to flow into schemes for developing the national resources of Britain.

Everything points at the present time to a slow but certain industrial change coming over Britain which will require considerable capital to carry through successfully. It is a significant fact that the unemployment figures for Britain, bad though they are, show no signs of getting worse, although there are seasonal fluctuations. Having regard to the steady increase of population, this would suggest that the aggregate volume of employment is slightly increasing. Further, the evidence tends to show that it is certain industries that are declining and others that are not only not declining, but actually going ahead. During the first seven months of the coal lock-out in 1926 Britain's export trade went down by £64 millions as compared with a similar period in 1925. But during that same period the basic or heavy industries—iron, steel, coal, and metallurgy—decreased their exports £71 millions, which suggests that industries other than basic must have increased their export by £7 millions, and that too under the most disadvantageous circumstances of the great industrial dispute. If one examines closer, one sees that the change is going on both geographically and according to industries. The Report of the Chief Factory Inspector for 1925 and 1926 [1] contains the following significant statement: "The general growth in an industrial sense of the southern area of the country, and particularly that of a part lying east of a line drawn from the Wash to Portsmouth, is again

[1] Cmd. 2714, 1926; Cmd. 2903, 1927.

noticeable. . . . The areas round London continue to develop in a remarkable manner. . . . In the Midland division the astonishing prosperity of Coventry and district is to be remarked on." Again, in the Report of the Ministry of Labour for 1926 [1] there is the following passage: "Certain observers profess to see in this irregular distribution of employment and unemployment a tendency for industrial development to move from the North towards the Midlands and South, and to turn from big establishments operating near the supplies of coal fuel to smaller establishments more widely scattered and drawing their power from electricity. Whether this is a true explanation of the currents in industrial expansion or not, there is no doubt that the Midlands and South and West have generally enjoyed greater prosperity, even in the difficult times of last year, and it is in those parts of the country that there has been occasional difficulty in obtaining labour of the right quality, although such labour clearly exists in other parts of the country." If one examines the *Ministry of Labour Gazette* for 1926, one finds that London and the South-Eastern area include nearly 25 per cent. of the total insured population of England and the four Southern divisions 46·4 per cent. of the total. Moreover, while between 1923 and 1926 the number of insured persons in industry rose by 5·1 per cent. in the Midlands and 11·58 per cent. in the South-Eastern area, it rose only 2·56 per cent. in the North-East, 3·41 per cent. in the North-West, and 1·92 per cent. in Wales. Or if one comes to consider employment according to occupation, still more striking figures can be obtained. The following is a list of the percentage increases between 1923 and 1926 of insured persons according to industry:—

[1] Cmd. 2856, Stationery Office.

Industry.	Southern Section, % Increase or Decrease.	Northern Section, % Increase or Decrease.
Oil, Grease, Glue, Soap, Ink, and Matches ..	+ 10·2	— 1·7
Paper and Paper Board	+ 1·1	— 1·2
Musical Instruments	+ 27·9	+ 6·7
Constructional Engineering	+ 26·9	+ 10·4
Silk (including Artificial Silk)	+ 38·7	+ 30·9
Furniture and Upholstering	+ 17·5	+ 10·6
Motor Industry, Cycles, and Air Craft ..	+ 17·4	+ 11·5
Brick, Tile, Cement, and Concrete ..	+ 35·7	+ 31·3
General Ironfounding	+ 8·4	+ 5·7
Distributive Trades	+ 31·1	+ 19·5
Coal Mining	— 8·4	— 2·4
Pig Iron Manufacture	— 14·9	— 16·8
General Engineering and Steel Founding ..	— 4·6	— 10·1
Marine Engineering	No change	— 15·7
Leather Industry	— 2·0	— 28·0

From this table we are struck by two facts. Firstly, that the Northern Section of England is progressing as regards industrial employment much slower than the Southern Section. Secondly, that the industries which produce the basic raw material for the finishing and specialized manufacturing trades have been going steadily back, while the latter have been going steadily forward. One of the largest increases of insured employment is in the Distributive, where no less than 260,000 more persons were employed during the period under review than in the previous period. This indicates that the food and drink industry is expanding. Possibly this may be due to a slight increase in the general standard of living of the population, as Professor Bowley and Sir J. Stamp suggest in their publication,[1] and possibly also the number is increasing of people who have retired from service or business in the

[1] *Op. cit.*

Empire and foreign countries and are living on pensions or savings in England. This would show itself in a rise in the food and drink industry. Probably, also, it is partly caused by an increase of luxury expenditure by the well-to-do. But quite apart from this there is strong evidence of a change-over in the centre of gravity of industry from the heavies to specialized manufactures. Most significant in this respect is the change that has taken place in the Midlands round Birmingham, and this is described by M. G. C. Allen in an article in the *Nation* for February 26, 1927. Birmingham was once the centre of an industrial area which produced coal, heavy iron goods, small metal wares, jewellery, hardware. These industries had been built up on the economic situation in Europe which arose after the Napoleonic wars. The changes which began already to be discernible in the seventies of last century culminated in the event of the Great War, "which of all others did most to confirm the direction of the new stream of forces." The growth of native industries abroad has largely killed the old Birmingham hardware export trade, the world crisis in the coal industry has knocked out the Black Country, while cheap Belgian steel undersells the products of the South Staffordshire iron industry. To escape the high transport charges and reduce costs the heavy industries have shifted from the Midlands to the coast. But in their place have sprung up gradually, almost imperceptibly, a whole host of new industries. "The roller and tube mills in the non-ferrous trades have found markets in the motor and motor-accessories industry, while the weldless steel-tube trade, which in pre-war days was mainly concerned with the boiler tubes for the shipbuilders, now looks to the cycle trade as its chief market. Many foundries which previously specialized in hollow ware now devote themselves partly to the production of castings for the electrical and light engineering trade. . . . In some old centres of the iron trade, such as Wolverhampton and Dudley, industries of a type quite new to the area, such as artificial silk and ready-made clothing industries, have been established. . . . The prosperity of the area has been maintained by the rise of industries engaged in producing motors, cycles, rubber goods, artificial silk, electrical equipment, machine tools, wireless apparatus, food and drink. These products are all of a highly finished kind and many of them of a highly composite nature."

Another indication of the industrial change is furnished by a table of industrial profits published by *The Times Trade and Engineering Supplement*, 1927. According to this, from 1920 to 1926 the profits from representative coal and metallurgical companies fell from 5·1 per cent. to a loss of 2·3 per cent.; in general engineering from 10·6 per cent. to 6·9 per cent.; in cotton industry from 8·1 per cent. to 7·9 per cent.; in wool from 8 per cent. to 1·9 per cent.; in shipping from 8·6 per cent. to 5 per cent.; while profits rose in the electrical manufacturing industries from 8·8 per cent. to 10·3 per cent.; in electrical power and supply from 8·2 per cent. to 11·2 per cent.; in chemical industries from 9·4 per cent. to 11·6 per cent.; in soap from 8·4 per cent. to 9·7 per cent. Particularly noticeable is the rise of the electrical industry. This is the herald of the new industrial revolution. Moreover, its expansion is not internal only, but the exports of electrical machinery have risen steadily, so that they are now well above the pre-war level both in volume and in value.

The driving force of the industrial changes coming over Britain, and, indeed, over all Western Europe, is to be found in the discoveries of science, which, as always in history, determine the economic and, ultimately, the social and political structure of human relations. The developments connected with the commercial application of recent industrial processes are roughly four in number. The first concerns the utilization of coal, and is likely to revolutionize the whole fuel problem. The second concerns electricity, and is likely to revolutionize the problem of power, and partly also that of transport. The third feature in the region of electro-chemical discovery is that of the fixation of nitrogen from the air by the so-called Haber process. A fourth is the manufacture of artificial silk by chemical processes out of wood fibre, which bids fair to modify and possibly rejuvenate the textile industry.

In regard to the new processes of coal utilization it is perhaps still early to speak of successful commercial application of all of them. Nevertheless two new methods have left the region of theory and are now in commercial use. One is the utilization of coal dust as a most efficient power producer with low ash percentage. According to the evidence of Dr. Rudolf Lessing before the Coal Commission in 1926, 25 million tons of incombustible material are hauled along the British railways every year. The utilization of dust and the conversion of coal on the spot into higher combustible material will be an enormous economy and reduce costs of production. Also the science of boiler making has advanced so far as to make it possible to economize fuel and increase power by the so-called superheating of steam. These processes are already in application and have, along with other causes, played a rôle in reducing the demand for coal as fuel in the raw state. Thus the depression in the old industry of mining and transporting from place to place coal in the raw is being to some extent

counterbalanced by the rise of new industries concerned with the more efficient use of coal and its
transformation into valuable chemical by-products.
The German scientist Dr. Bergius and others have
done a lot of research which should still further
revolutionize the fuel industry. In a conference on
coal utilization at Pittsburg in 1926, Dr. Bergius
stated that he estimated that he could produce 45s.
worth of fuel-oil from a piece of coal worth 15s. The
problem, however, appears not so simple as that
bald statement would imply, because it has yet to be
shown that the cost of conversion by distillation of
coal under high pressure in powerful retorts does not
eat up the difference between the 15s. and the 45s.
Still, in Germany they believe they have found a
solution which is commercially applicable, and the
great German Dye Trust, in its works at Merseburg,
has been engaged for some time in manufacturing
synthetic petrol from coal. It is hoped from these
works to turn out a million barrels a year and eventually
to make Germany independent of foreign importation
of the mineral-oil products. In general it may be said
that since the end of the inflation period in Germany
the electro-chemical industry represented by the German Dye Trust has replaced in economic and political
influence the coal and steel interests, personified as
they were between 1920 and 1924 in the Stinnes
Trust, now in liquidation. This indicates that the
industrial changes are affecting the continent of
Europe to quite the same extent as Great Britain.

Arising out of the process of converting coal into
liquid and gaseous fuel comes the second change
concerning the extension of cheap electric power.
Speaking recently before the Institution of Civil
Engineers, Professor Douglas Hay said: "Taken as
a whole, the generating capacity of colliery stations

was greater than was usually realized, and the general experience of these stations was that it was possible to produce energy at or below o·3d. per unit. . . . In the case of colliery groups which work coking coals, the trend of practice was towards the installation of a large central coke-oven and by-product plants, in conjunction with which a power station would be operated to consume waste fuels. It should be possible to sell to bulk consumers after simple transformation from the high-pressure transmission at less than o·4d. per unit. Such a figure would materially affect the electrification of railways and the heavy industries. . . . The future of such schemes must depend upon the ability of the community to absorb both the surplus gas and the surplus electricity." Thus we see here that a large field is open for the investment of capital at home for the purpose of providing cheap electric power for the public and for industry, whereby a great cheapening of the cost of production would be effected and the export trade indirectly assisted.

The third new process has had less practical application in Britain than in Germany, where the fixation of nitrogen from the air by the Haber process has made that country independent of imported Chilian nitrates and has played an immense rôle in providing cheap fertilizers for German agriculture. But beginnings have been made by the Imperial Chemical Industries, which is playing the same rôle in British industrial life as the German Dye Trust, and which perhaps is destined in time to acquire the same predominance over coal, iron, and steel as its German counterpart has over the Westphalian heavy industries.

There is enough evidence now to assure us that the internal capital market of Britain could be profitably employed for some years to come in supplying the financial means for carrying out the new industrial revolution. All the more is this the case if a national policy is developed for agriculture, and if by a system of National Import Boards the price of the staple agricultural commodities is stabilized and speculation eliminated. One agricultural authority has estimated that under a better system of marketing the produce of the soil of England could be increased in value by £100 millions. It would be a great mistake, however, to imagine that Britain could by this process even approximate towards becoming a self-supporting country. Even after imports have been cut down to the bare necessities, even after internal development schemes have raised the production of the soil at home, there will remain a large amount of food and raw material to be paid for by foreign investments or by commodity exports. Certain articles of agricultural produce must always be grown cheaper in the prairie countries of America and Asia than in the older countries of Europe, with their higher production costs. In Britain agriculture is attempting to get over its difficulties by specializing in the production of the higher grades of articles of food in which the prairie lands cannot so well compete—such as milk, "baby beef," and early lamb. In the staple articles of food Britain must always be a large importer, and therefore cannot do without an export trade to balance her accounts. In fact, Britain, while she ought to concentrate on providing capital for internal industrial reconstruction, ought to do so with one eye upon the need of this reconstruction to improve the export trade in the new articles for which the coming industrial revolution will provide a market abroad. If the dominions in future mine their own coal and build their own railways more and more, if the Chinese and Indians weave their own cheap cloths, Britain can supply them in future with motor-cars, cycles, wireless sets, electrical plants, and the numerous other articles which under the present conditions of the world can only be produced cheaply and efficiently in an old industrial country with a high technical efficiency and with generations of skilled labour behind it. The argument is sometimes used by those who would concentrate solely on raising the purchasing power of the home consumers by living wages and family allowances that mass production for the home market would make it possible to sell cheap for the export market and so re-establish the competitive position of Britain. While the raising of the standard of living of the working classes would have the best possible effect in improving the home market and the position of some industries, it must not be forgotten that the effect would be felt only in those industries which supply the public with goods for immediate consumption. This would apply to the food and drink trade, the clothing and the leather trade. For the more wages a British worker gets and the higher his family allowances, the more food, clothes, and boots he can buy. But unfortunately that will not enable Britain to pay for its indispensable imports. Boots and clothes turned out under mass production for the home market cannot be dumped cheaply abroad to pay for raw cotton, rubber, and wool. The Egyptian "fellah" who grows the cotton and the Malayan planter who grows the rubber do not want the clothes and boots that are put on the British home market: the "fellah" wears sandals and the planter alpaca coats, which are probably more cheaply supplied by Japan. But both of them may be induced to buy wireless sets and cycles. The raising of the purchasing power of the British working class will not have effect on the condition of trade unless it is also accompanied by the rise in the purchasing power of the coloured

N

millions in Asia and Africa, who are as indispensable
customers of British industry as are the British workers.
Everything seems to point towards small special industries, rather than large mass-production industries, as
the most effective means of providing for the export
trade of Britain.

In this connection it is interesting to hear a well-
informed American journalist, Mr. Raymond Swing,
in a series of articles in the *Philadelphia Public Ledger*,
comparing the different methods of production in
England and the United States. "Given a population
of over 100 million people," he writes, "and natural
resources in great abundance, the American technique
of mass production is the natural and right one. But
it is another question whether this technique is
suitable to an island Empire which does not supply
half its own food and must purchase the bulk of its
raw material. Such a nation must pay for what it
buys and must sell its goods all over the world. Mass
production means a standardized article, and most
manufactures can be standardized only where the
population is homogeneous, as in America. The
British cannot pay for their food and raw materials
by selling to themselves. They must sell over a wide
range of diverse markets, where standardization is
impossible. More than that, they must build up their
whole business on the basis of making specialities
for special needs. The great American manufacturer
can work on a different scheme. He can assure himself
of his profit by first selling to his home market.
He has covered his risks at home. What he sells abroad
is 'velvet.' Only in that way can standardized goods
be sold abroad. Only when the people in India, China,
Russia, South America, and Africa want substantially
the same articles could England reconstruct her
export manufactures on a mass-production basis."

Mr. Swing gives an example of a Lancashire textile firm which prints a special kind of calico with a Landseer scene on it, in which the colours overlap one another, so as to spoil the artistic effect. This kind of calico, and this alone, is demanded by natives of a certain part of Africa, because they have always been used to it, and the machines have to be regularly stopped and this special print turned out for this market. It is obvious that the limits of standardization are reached in England, and for that matter in Western Europe, much quicker than in the United States.

It would seem, therefore, that the future development of Western and Central Europe in general, and of Great Britain in particular, should be along parallel lines of (1) re-establishing the home market by raising the purchasing power of the masses; (2) pushing of export trade by assisting the rise of the standard of living of the Asiatic and African coolie populations; (3) the acceleration of the industrial revolution going on at home by a judicious application under State control of a portion of the nation's savings in new schemes of internal development. In Germany much has already been done for the covering of the country with a network of electrical systems, and for this purpose national trusts have been formed with public and private capital. In Britain barely a beginning has been made, but it is long overdue, and one of the first measures of a progressive administration should be to raise an internal loan for national reconstruction. By this method the private capitalist would become a bondholder and take his fixed interest, while the profits derived from this industrial regeneration would accrue to the community.

CHAPTER XIII

PROGRESS BY EVOLUTION OR CATASTROPHE?

IN our review of world economy since the war we have directed special attention to Europe and to Britain in particular, and we have seen a distinct tendency since, roughly, 1922 for monetary and industrial affairs to stabilize round a certain average production, circulation, and general activity. We have seen that the war greatly magnified and accelerated certain tendencies which had set in even before 1914, and that it caused political revolutions in Central Europe, a social revolution in Russia, and widespread currency disturbances, through inflation and the expropriating of bondholders, over a large part of the Continent. From the close of the war to the summer of 1920 it looked as if these economic dislocations would generate such social unrest that catastrophic developments, like those which had taken place in Russia, would extend to a large part of Europe. The seizure of factories by the Italian workers, the march of the Russian Red Army on Warsaw in 1920, the growth of the Communist movement in Germany, and the coming to power of a working-class Government in Saxony in 1923, all seemed to point to rapid social changes. But towards the end of 1923, in Central Europe, and earlier in Italy and in Eastern Europe, signs were not wanting of the ebb of the revolutionary wave. Undoubtedly the intervention of the international money-lending houses in London and New York played a big rôle in bringing about the change. The cruder forms of French Imperialism was curbed, the control of the war-time profiteer over the victorious

Governments was loosened, and the Government of
the United States was induced to take an interest in
Europe. American finance "returned to Europe," and
in the American Relief Administration Mr. Hoover
suppressed Bolshevism by stuffing the mouths of the
hungry proletariat of Central Europe with food. Sir
William Goode, that indiscreet mouthpiece of the
Hungarian dictator, frankly admitted that relief works
in Europe had mainly a political object, in a letter to
The Times on October 12, 1925. "Food," he wrote,
"was practically the only basis on which the Governments of the hastily created States could be maintained in power. . . . If it had not been for the
£137 millions in relief credits granted to Central and
Eastern Europe between 1919 and 1921, it would
have been impossible to provide food and coal and
the land and sea transport for them. Without food
and coal and transport, Austria, and probably several
countries, would have gone the way of Russia. In
the chaos that then prevailed the problem was not
to draw up irreproachable protocols for currency
stabilization and financial control, but to find an
engine to take you to the country, and to find a Government when you got there. Two and a half years after
the Armistice, and after the back of Bolshevism in
Central Europe had been broken, largely by relief
credits, the League of Nations began to tackle Austria."

But if Europe has entered calmer political waters,
if, as Trotsky put it, "America has put Europe on
rations," if a certain atmosphere of stability seems
to have been created, it must not be forgotten that
nothing in economics or politics is static. The forces
that make for change, as far as Western and Central
Europe are concerned, may not be pushing the
Continent into the Russian cataract, but they certainly
are not allowing it to remain in a stagnant backwater.

There was probably something more needed than the food credits and the financial intervention of America to prevent a break-up. Deep-seated cultural and economic causes were at work as well. Europe, from the Atlantic seaboard to the Eastern frontiers of Germany, Czecho-Slovakia, and Austria, is, roughly speaking, one cultural whole in comparison to what lies to the east of this line. The ancient customs of the Holy Roman Empire, the Roman laws of landed property, the tradition of the Catholic Church, the cult of individual character, peasant proprietorship, the rise of a highly complex industrial and financial system and of an intricate network of commercial exchange, gave Western and Central Europe a social and economic fabric which, though shaken by the war and by the after-war chaos, was not wrecked, as were the fabrics of society farther to the East. One has only to look at pre-war Russia to realize how incapable that country was of standing a long and unsuccessful war. Primitive Slav communes in the villages, an agrarian nobility exercising the authority of mediæval serf-proprietors, an autocracy which was founded originally to provide a centralized force against the Tartar hordes, but whose function was now superfluous, an absence of industrial areas over a large part of the country, and an almost complete dependence on foreign finance—all these factors made Russia incapable of the strain of prolonged war and caused after the third winter a complete collapse of the ordinary comforts of civilization. Everything was prepared for the social revolution, not by what the agitators preached from below, but by what the old order and the historical past of Russia accumulated from above.

Still, the fact remains that if the Great War had continued for some time longer, Russian catastrophic conditions might have spread westwards. Moreover, if another war, worse and more devastating than the last, were to break out in Europe in the future, it is more than probable that the process of gradual evolution along the lines of increasing socialization of essentially social services will come to an end and an era of chaos set in, out of which anything may come, from a Bolshevik revolution to a Fascist dictatorship. It is important to consider whether a war is likely to break out in the world in the near future, and if so what are the chances of its localization. Arising out of this we ought to consider what are the factors, social and economic, that create conditions favourable to wars. It is largely upon this question of whether war breaks out in Europe or elsewhere in the world involving Europe, that the fate of the present relative stabilization in Western and Central Europe and of the gradual change which is accompanying it will be decided. The importance of considering this question in relation to Western and Central Europe cannot be over-estimated. For it is the Old World which still carries with it centuries of accumulated cultural traditions. It is the little continent of Europe, this Western offshoot of the Asiatic land mass, which has the oldest, most experienced, and skilled workmen and a specialized industrial system, that can set a standard to the whole world. It is Europe, excluding the Slav countries which border Asia, that has given this great tradition to the English-speaking continent of America. It is the United States, Great Britain, Germany, Belgium, and Northern France that provide the chief industrial power-belt in the world. The United States and Great Britain alone control 75 per cent. of the world's mineral production. The concentration of the greatest industrial areas of the world round the seaboard of the North Atlantic is due to the existence in this area of

immense deposits of coal and iron, together with the
necessary additions of copper, lead, zinc, oil, and other
minerals. Thanks to this, the North Atlantic countries
are doing annually five times the mechanical work
of Russia, China, and India, the three most populous
areas of the Old World outside Western Europe.
The former countries have one-fifth of the world's
population, but do about two-fifths of the world's
work. This is due to the fortunate association of
minerals, combined with favourable healthy and
temperate climatic conditions. Other regions have
not these favourable circumstances. Thus, China has
large resources of coal but no iron. The East Indies
have iron but no coal. India has iron but no suitable
coking coal in adequate quantities. Japan has neither
coal nor iron in sufficient quantities. It has coal in
Manchuria, but it has not the iron resources yet.
The countries bordering the Mediterranean have
neither coal nor iron in the necessary amounts. The
only areas in the world where the mineral bases of
an industrial civilization outside the North Atlantic
countries are to be found are in Australia, South
Africa, and Southern Russia. But even here the
resources will, in time, only be enough to supply
the growing populations of these areas, and not enough
to provide for the rest of the world. Western Europe,
therefore, and North America are likely to remain
the most important forces, economically and politically,
in the world for a long time to come. A gradual social
evolution towards industrial democracy in these countries will have important influences on the rest of the
world. A breakdown of this evolution would mean
the paralysis of the world's greatest industrial area,
and another war would bring it to the brink of this
breakdown.

Yet it is undoubtedly true that the eastern side of

the North Atlantic industrial area, namely, Western and Central Europe, is an area of the world where ancient religious feuds, which have their roots in past ages, and national animosities, which were characteristic of an earlier phase of capitalistic society, are still strong. It is possible that an economic breakdown in the eastern end of the North Atlantic industrial area will be caused by war, brought about by some, as yet unhealed, national or cultural quarrel in Europe. Speaking generally, there are three kinds of war. The first is between two highly or relatively highly industrialized Powers, where capital accumulation is going on. These would be the A and B type of country.[1] A war between countries of this kind would be waged over the possession of spheres of influence in some weaker country of the D and E type. Such a war would be the late war, as far as it concerned England and France on the one side and Germany on the other. It is commonly known as the Imperialist type of war. The second kind of war is between two countries with low industrial organization, small capital accumulation, and large agrarian population of the D category, and is generally fought over administrative posts in still weaker countries, such as those in category E.[2] An example of this were the Balkan wars of 1912 and 1913, where religious animosity and national passions from bygone centuries were used to exploit the interests of ambitious rulers. Another example were the Russo-Turkish wars of last century and the struggle over Constantinople, whereby also the agrarian nobility of Russia and Turkey contended for lucrative posts in administrative provinces in Armenia and Asia Minor. The third kind of war is between the areas of capital accumulation (A and B categories) and colonial countries (D and E categories).

[1] See Chapter IV. [2] Ibid.

These can be called colonial wars, wars of national liberation, and revolutionary wars. An example of this would be the French wars in Morocco and Syria, the British expedition to China in 1926, and the conflict between the British and the Chinese Nationalist movement, the civil wars in Russia between 1918 and 1920, whereby the victorious Entente Powers (categories A and B) through White armies tried to interfere by force with the revolutionary and in part national movement in Russia in the interest of foreign finance and investment.

From this we can see that the causes of some wars are economic and of some non-economic. As regards the first type of war, the economic cause was demonstrated by the Versailles Treaty in so far as it concerned the settlement between England, France, and Germany. We have studied in Chapter VIII the economic aims and effects of this treaty. As regards the third or colonial type of war, the motive of Imperialist expansion on the part of the A and B type of country is also economic. On the other hand, we saw in Chapter VII, in discussing the causes of the Great War, that the danger-point round which the conflict grew was not between England and Germany, not between the A and B types, but between countries in the D category, Russia and the old Austro-Hungarian Empire, the countries of the low capital accumulation. Thus it is necessary to recognize that the second type of war may be engendered by motives which are not primarily economic. The question arises: could any of these wars break out in Europe or elsewhere in the world in the near future? and if so, which of these three types of wars is the most likely to break out?

Let us examine the possibility of wars of the first type—the Imperialist war. We have seen in Chapter IX that the tendency is increasing in the highly industrialized countries (A and B types) for international agreements in certain branches of industry to be made, whereby markets are agreed upon, production, prices, and export quotas regulated. The international "Cartel" is certainly something which has come to stay, and if it stays and extends it will reduce very largely the incentives to seek for market outlets by force of arms. Capital invested in industry is always inclined to favour aggressive foreign policies, because wars, amongst other things, generally enrich the captains of industry by raising prices. If, however, in the field of industry the pace is being set for international agreement, this is all the more the case in the field of finance. Banking and bondholder capital is always the loser by wars and inflation which comes with wars, and the possibility of recouping losses by reparations payments from the vanquished country is, as we have seen in Chapter X, a very doubtful proposition. The disappearance of Germany as an uncontrolled unit of industrial and finance capital has removed one danger of war. The tendency is now towards Franco-German *rapprochement*, which is a plant of tender and slow, but apparently of sure, growth. The possibility of Anglo-French hostile developments may also be excluded on the grounds of there being no areas where friction, due to colonial expansion and the export of commodities and capital, is likely to arise. French industry is participating in the industrial agreements which the after-war period has produced, and French finance is interested in keeping on good terms with London and New York in order to stabilize the franc, for France is still largely a bondholder country, for whom war means severe losses whichever way it goes. The possibilities of war between England and America may be excluded, if only because the United States is so vastly superior in strategic advantage that it could damage the British Empire at one blow by the annexation of Canada. Besides, in spite of friction over oil, rubber, and the products of tropical areas of which the British Empire possesses a monopoly, there is too much American bondholder capital invested in Britain, and too much British bondholder capital in the United States to make war an attractive proposition. Imperialist wars of the first A and B categories are therefore very unlikely in the present state of the world. The only danger which may arise is from the possible resurrection of the military power of Germany. This is within the bounds of possibility if Great Britain, France, the United States, and Japan do not in the course of the next decade take practical steps towards disarmament. One other danger-point, not directly affecting Europe, however, is in the Far East, and concerns the relations between the United States and Japan. In Chapter IV, I classed Japan in C, but she will soon be in B category. There are no industrial agreements and interlocking investments between these two countries as yet, and competition for spheres of interest in China, combined with coloured-labour problems in the Western States of America, may cause complications. Time will undoubtedly solve this problem by bringing a rise in the standard of living of yellow labour, and the best guarantee for this is a strong trade-union movement in Japan. But the question may be rightly asked if these developments may not be too slow to prevent war danger from developing.

Coming to the second type of war, we find that there is more material for this type of conflagration than there is for the first type. When Mussolini spoke of making the air dark with Italian aeroplanes, he was probably indulging in a boast, which is characteristic of his movement and which seeks to hide weakness behind big talk. But Italy, at present in C category, is in a transition state from a semi-agrarian country, priest-ridden and with a high birth-rate, to a country with some newly-accumulated industrial capital in the North, producing goods quicker than the impoverished and rapidly increasing population can consume. Italy is in the early stages of capital accumulations, and is not yet brought fully into the international financial network. Her industrialists may therefore be able to force the pace, and bring on a war with a neighbour in B category, like France, or with a colonial country in D category, like Yugoslavia, which is climbing gradually into C. Moreover, in countries of early accumulation of capital, non-economic motives, reflecting the psychology of an earlier economic phase, are often influential in moulding policy. The megalomania of Mussolini, and his idea of reviving the ancient Roman Empire, may reflect the desire of a military and bureaucratic caste in Rome, just as it did in pre-revolutionary Russia and the old Austro-Hungarian Empire for lucrative governorships in annexed Turkish provinces. The danger of war in the East Mediterranean, while real, can undoubtedly be prevented if the countries of the high capital accumulation, and therefore of the higher military and naval power, are united and determined to prevent, or at least to localize, it.

As regards the third or colonial type of war, it is well to remember that we have already had numerous doses of little wars of this type since the Great War. The examples are the Russian civil wars, the French wars in Morocco and Syria, the British actions in Egypt and China, the Mexican civil wars, and the United States intervention in Nicaragua. At one time in 1925 it looked as if there was going to be a distinct line-up of world economic and political forces, whereby Western Europe and North America would be on one side, representing the countries of high capital accumulation, and the colonial areas of Eastern Asia (China), Near East (Turkey and Syria), North Africa, and Central America (Mexico), under the moral leadership of Soviet Russia, would be on the other. Undoubtedly there is a strong economic basis for a world orientation of this kind, because it contains capital-exporting countries, on the one hand, desiring political control over the economically undeveloped countries on the other. But so far there has not been anything like a united front on either side. There is no united front of the European Powers and America against China. The United States and Britain follow quite different tactics in relation to the Chinese national movement. There is no united front against Russia in a naval and military sense, and no evidence that any of the Powers are contemplating a return to the disgraceful and ill-fated expeditions in support of Russian White armies. It is true there is a financial blockade of Soviet Russia, whereby the latter is prevented from borrowing on the European Stock Exchanges, but even here this is not strictly kept, as witness the German short-term commercial credits to Russia. The Soviet Union is undoubtedly a disturbing factor to the countries of high capital accumulation. First of all its presence in Asia endangers the political privileges of the ruling Anglo-Indian caste and the British monopoly rights in the Chinese treaty ports. Secondly, its internal reconstruction programmes, giving precedence to the rights of labour, nationalizing the key industries and transport, putting foreign trade under State monopoly and generally attempting to introduce an ordered plan, where unregulated private moneyed interests used to profiteer

at the public expense before, have all tended to render it anathema to the political, industrial, and financial chiefs of Europe and America. On the other hand, it has awakened sympathy among the Labour and Socialist movements all over Europe and among the Nationalist movements in Asia.

Thanks to this kind of moral isolation in which the Powers of Western Europe and America have kept Russia, the leaders of the Soviet Union have tended to develop a doctrinaire fanaticism which endows their movement with something in the nature of a religious crusade, reminiscent of the early stages of Islam. The idea of proselytizing and converting the world to the conception of the World Revolution arises largely out of the underground activities to which the Russian revolutionary leaders were for years condemned under the Tsars' regime. The Communist International is a product of these conditions, intensified by the Great War, which made the Russian Revolution inevitable in the form that it took and created converts by the thousand to the idea of a catastrophic collapse of the old society, on the ruins of which the new alone could be born. But just as there is no united front of the Imperialist Powers against Russia and against the colonial national movements in Asia, so there is no united front of the latter against the Imperialist Powers. The events of 1927 showed that the National movement in China was divided, and that the greater part of it had not accepted the rigorous doctrines of the Communist International. The Mexican revolutionary movement has kept definitely aloof from either the old West European or the Communist International and is undecided whether to follow the traditions of the Labour movements of North America, Western Europe, or Russia. In Russia herself the history of the

Revolution since the days of Lenin's famous stra-
tegical retreat to the "New Economic Policy" in 1921
has been a steady series of compromises, first with
the Russian peasantry and small proprietor-cultivators,
and then with foreign capital, which under certain
very definite conditions is now allowed to operate
inside the Soviet Union. The necessity to permit
private accumulations of capital in the hands of the
peasantry alongside of State accumulations,[1] and the
desire to accelerate the rate of national reconstruction
by attracting foreign capital into Russia, has brought
the Soviet leaders up against the whole problem
of the Communist International. This was founded,
as we noted above, on the traditions of a time now
past, namely, of the subterranean existence under
Tsardom and of the civil wars and foreign interven-
tions in the early phase of the Revolution. An entirely
paradoxical situation is thus produced. If foreign
capital is to be called in and the financial blockade of
Russia is to be broken down, if a settlement of the
Tsarist debt problems is to be made by the writing
down of the latter and the securing of a Reconstruction Loan from the European money markets, it is
obviously impossible for the Soviet leaders to sanction
activities of the Communist International in their
present form, which are based on the assumption
that European economy is on the eve of collapse.
If they want this form of reconstruction, they must
do something to create an atmosphere of conciliation,
and act on the assumption that the economic system
of the Soviet Union can live together in a world
where private enterprise is still dominant, though
retreating by slow stages. The dual policy of Russia
to-day is well seen in the fact that, while the Soviet
delegation comes to Geneva to take part in the dis-

[1] See Chapter XI.

cussion at the World Economic Conference, the Russian Communist leaders are running a campaign of military "preparedness" and acting on the assumption that Europe is on the brink of war. This war psychology is a reflection of a desire of a section of Soviet leaders to justify the existence of the Communist International, and to perpetuate the mentality born of the illegality of Tsarist days and in the fever of the revolutionary wars against Denikin and Koltchak. It is necessary for European public opinion to be patient, to curb those who still cannot realize that the revolutionary regime in Russia has come to stay, and to wait for the inevitable trend of events which will make the "realists" in Moscow mould the foreign policy of the Soviet Union.

A colonial war with Europe and America on one side, and Russia, Asia, and North Africa on the other, is fit food for the sensational novelist, but there is no reason why it should come to pass. A whole literature has sprung up among the Socialist movements of the Continent which aims at showing that this kind of war is inevitable. The idea is based on the theory of the connection between the modern capitalist States and the export of capital to colonial areas. The German revolutionary, Rosa Luxemburg, in a great work,[1] sought to show that systems of private capital accumulation could not exist unless these accumulations were exported and invested in undeveloped countries, and that stability was not possible until the colonies are all developed, when a catastrophic breakdown, heralding the social revolution, was inevitable. Lenin, on the other hand, in various works published in his lifetime, and Bukharin in a recent publication,[2] sought to show that capitalist society

[1] *Akkumulation des Kapitals.* Frankes Vertag, Leipzig, 1921.
[2] *Imperialismus und Akkumulation des Kapitals.* Vienna, 1926.

must create, even before the colonial areas of the earth
are all developed, crises of production and consumption
which must lead to an upheaval of the working class
and a collapse of the existing system of economy.
Rosa Luxemburg postulated the export of capital to
areas which no longer required it, and consequent
under-consumption of commodities at home, because
capital was not being invested in home production.
From this followed violent attempts to force the
already developed colonies to take more capital,
with consequent widespread colonial wars, chaos, and
revolutions. Lenin and Bukharin postulated lack of
proportion between the different branches of capitalist
production, and not under-consumption, as the cause
of inevitable breakdown. They saw in the inability of
the over-expanded heavy industries of Europe and
America to find the necessary markets the bankruptcy
of the old industrial system, the inability to provide
wages for the masses, and consequent progressive
attacks on the standard of living, calling forth revolutionary upheaval. Those who have followed the history
of the economic development since the war, as given
in the above pages, will see that both these two schools
of continental Socialists are partly right and both
partly wrong. Luxemburg was right in maintaining
that the export of capital to colonial areas, if unrestricted by public interest, must lead to under-consumption at home and political complications abroad.
Lenin and Bukharin were right, that the heavy industries
of the world have reached a productive capacity far in
excess of the world's consuming capacity. But Luxemburg was on dangerous ground in assuming that the
export of capital cannot be controlled in the public
interest without a catastrophe and revolution, and
that the highly industrialized States of Western and
Central Europe and North America will not in the

course of this generation find a way to regulate the investment of national savings, so that they may cease to create the danger of under-consumption at home and colonial wars abroad. It remains to be seen if these countries succeed in finding a way of curbing the moneyed interests without a violent upheaval, and in directing those investments which are not needed abroad for the purchase of the necessary food and raw material to the home market for industrial reconstruction and for the raising of the consuming power of the people at home and abroad. Lenin and Bukharin were wrong in assuming that necessarily there will be a catastrophic collapse of the industries of the highly organized States, because of the disequilibrium between "construction" and "consumption" industries. It is, as we have seen in Chapter IX, within the bounds of possibility that international industrial agreements will regulate production of the "heavies" and bring it in line with other branches of industry. Once again, and in conclusion, it is not necessary to postulate catastrophe in order that Mankind shall work his way out of the disorders of unregulated production and distribution to a more rational system of economy in the world after the Great War.

INDEX

For Product Safety Concerns and Information please contact our EU
representative GPSR@taylorandfrancis.com
Taylor & Francis Verlag GmbH, Kaufingerstraße 24, 80331 München, Germany

www.ingramcontent.com/pod-product-compliance
Lightning Source LLC
Chambersburg PA
CBHW061211220326
41599CB00025B/4607